HAMPTON W

BRICK BY BRICK

The Building and Buildings of Hampton Wick 1750 - 2012

Volume 2: Park Road and environs

Ray Elmitt

HAMPTON WICK HISTORY NOVEMBER 2013

In memory of

Colin Pain 1928 - 2013

A deeply knowledgeable and infectiously enthusiastic
local historian
who set me on the path

I am always grateful for the help and encouragement I receive from fellow local history enthusiasts especially Kelvin Adams, Tony Arbour, Paul Barnfield, Mike Cherry, Martin Haskell, Ken Howe and John Shaef. Thanks also for the particular help I have had in the preparation of this volume from local residents including Alan Buckingham, Pamela Campbell (née Offer), David Peregrine Jones, Caroline Helm, Peter Holland, Anna Joyce, Keith and Kornelia Kelly, Tessa Mack, Margaret Markham, Alison and Mark Merrington, Andrea Morris, Richard Pain, Mary Ramsay, David Rees, Keith and Debbie Wagner, Malcolm Watton, Deryck and Margaret Winter. Finally I am pleased to acknowledge the assistance I have received from the staff of the Local Study Rooms in both Richmond upon Thames and Kingston upon Thames.

Copyright © 2013 Ray Elmitt.
The book author retains sole copyright to his contributions to this book.

The right of Ray Elmitt to be identified as the author of this work has been asserted by him in accordance with the Copyright, Design and Patents Act 1988

First published 2013 by
Hampton Wick History
1 The Grove, 24 Lower Teddington Road
Hampton Wick, Middlesex KT1 4HJ
website: www.hamptonwickhistory.org.uk
email: ray@hamptonwickhistory.org.uk

ISBN 978-0-9571679-4-0

The cover design is based on a section of the elegant 1936 brickwork of Ingram Court, Park Road

Contents

Part One: Discovering the Past

Part Two: Exploring the Present

Appendix:
The Brick by Brick Website

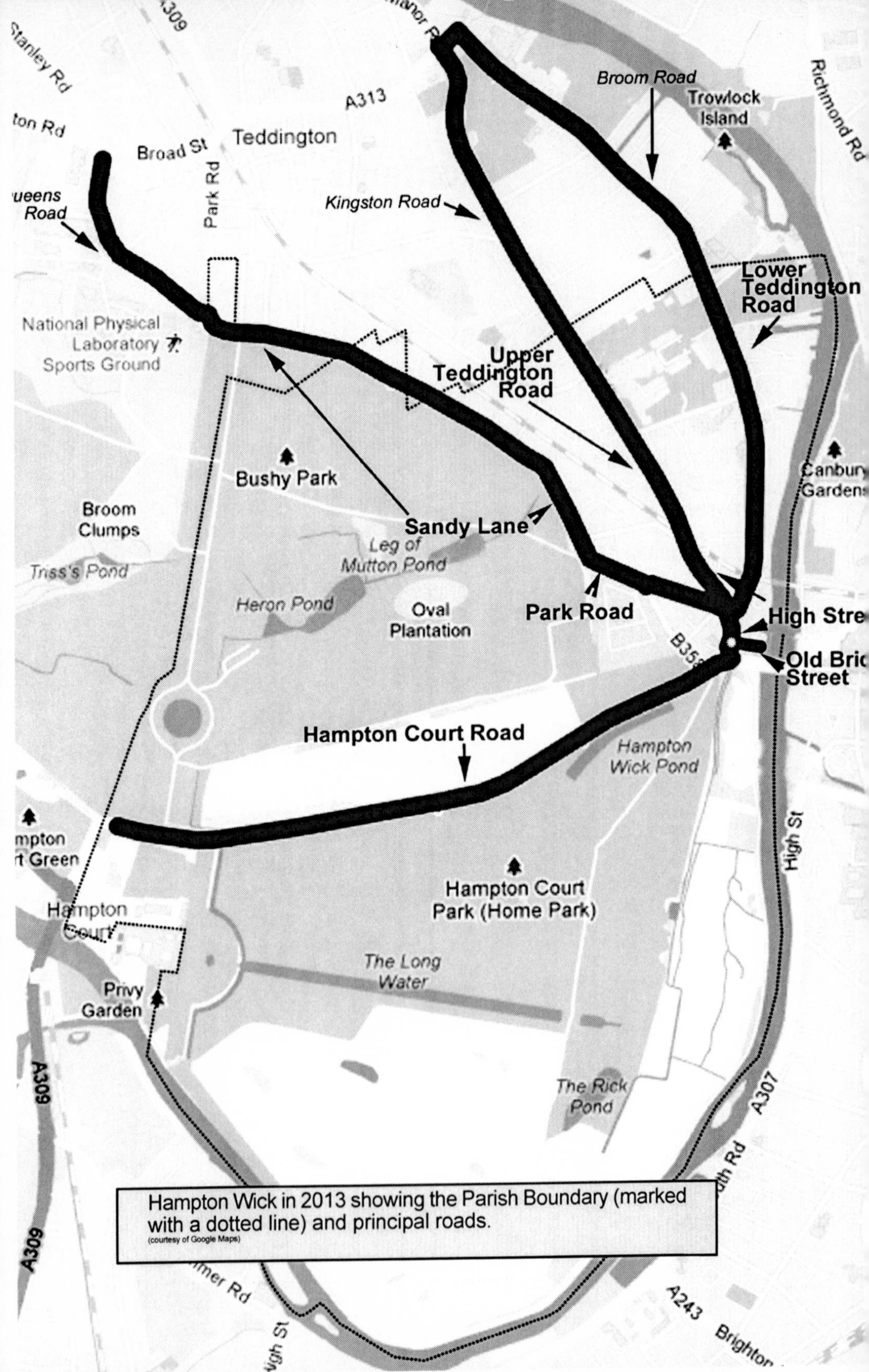

Hampton Wick in 2013 showing the Parish Boundary (marked with a dotted line) and principal roads.
(courtesy of Google Maps)

Series Introduction

Hampton Wick owes its importance to three factors: one geographic and two historic. First, it is located on the River Thames at a point where the riverbed provided a fordable crossing. Second, it is immediately opposite Kingston, historically an important market town where seven Saxon Kings were crowned. Third, it is close to (and was part of) the Manor of Hampton Court which was in existence from the time of the Domesday Book and which became increasingly prominent once Henry VIII had appropriated it from Cardinal Wolsey in 1528.

These three factors worked in combination with each other. The juxtaposition of both Kingston and Hampton Court created a natural flow of traffic between the two, which necessarily passed through the hamlet of Hampton Wick to use the ford and - from the end of the 12th century - the bridge. Travellers from further afield whose journey involved crossing the river were also funnelled through the hamlet because for five centuries this was the only bridge crossing between London Bridge to the east and Staines Bridge to the west.

However, while it enjoyed this unique position, Hampton Wick lacked autonomy because it fell within the larger parish of Hampton. This subservience was significant because the Wick and the Town (as the local population referred to the two entities) were physically separated by 900 acres of Royal Park. The long walk to St Mary's Church, Hampton on Sundays and Feast Days was a constant physical reminder of the Wick's lesser status. The division of proceeds from the Poor Rates - two-thirds to the Town and one-third to the Wick - was also a long-running grievance.

Around 1830 Hampton Wick was able to make its first bid for freedom. The fear of unrest within the growing population following the end of the Napoleonic Wars led the Government to fund the building

The establishment of the Parish Church of St John the Baptist, opened in 1830, gave Hampton Wick its own identity.

of several new churches. *St John the Baptist Church* in the Wick was originally opened in November 1830 as a chapel-at-ease for St Mary's, Hampton but the Bishop of London upgraded it to a full parish in July 1831, with its own vicar and its own precisely defined boundary (see page 8). The only setback was the stipulation that the existing split of the Poor Rates proceeds between the two communities must be maintained.

In 1863, the railway came to Hampton Wick via a branch line from Twickenham to Kingston. The following year Hampton received its railway connection but this was on the separate spur line out to Shepperton. Four stations and a change of train at Strawberry Hill now separated the "neighbours". This separation must have had an impact on the two communities as well as being a real consideration in the minds of the new generation of commuters.

The third and decisive break with Hampton also came in 1863 when the new Local Government Act allowed the Wick to establish its own Local Board that, amongst other powers, enabled it to retain and spend the proceeds of its own Poor Rates. By now Hampton Wick was experiencing an explosive growth both in population and in house-building, and the new-found independence of The Local Board empowered it to direct this more effectively. It was the practical question of how to dispose of the sewage - one of their direct responsibilities - that would prove the greatest challenge for the Board.

*

The physical layout of Hampton Wick reflects its origins. The river crossing made the bridge and its approach the focus of the village. (Old) Bridge Street and its junction with the High Street became the most densely populated area and at this point converged the four roads used by travellers passing through the Wick or using the crossing. The layout and road system is evident on the 1740 map (see page 8) on which the junction of the High Street with the road to the bridge is marked with an arrow.

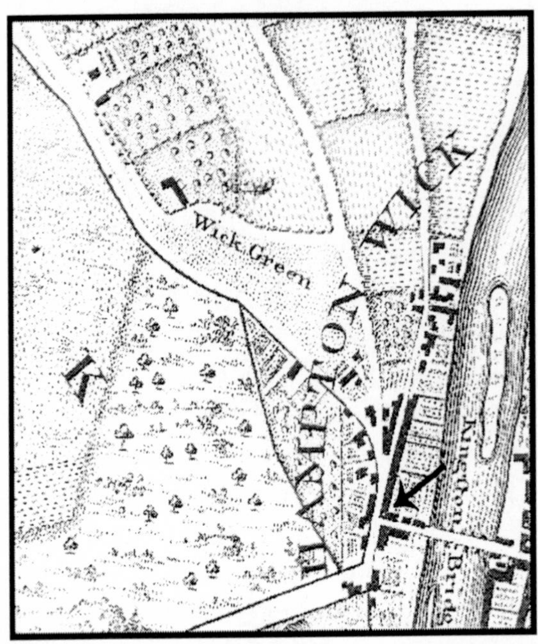

above Detail from Jean Rocque's Map of Hampton Court and Surrounds c1740. The arrow marks the junction of the main street and the road to the bridge from which the road system radiates.

below Description of the Boundary of Hampton Wick Parish

Numb. 18828. [1501]

The London Gazette.

Published by Authority.

TUESDAY, JULY 26, 1831.

The boundary to commence in the centre of the river Thames, at Kingston-bridge, where the hamlet of Hampton-wick joins the parish of Kingston, and to comprise the west side of the river, along the whole extent of the parish of Kingston to the parish of Thames-Ditton, where the river takes a direction westward; and the boundary then comprises the north side of the river, separating the district of Hampton-wick, from the parishes of Thames-Ditton and East Molesey, till it comes opposite to Hampton-court-palace, where it joins the town division of Hampton, and leaving the river goes up the centre of the Privy-gardens to the south front of the Palace, along which it proceeds eastward, and thence along the east front of the Palace northward, and returns westward up the Office-yard, and along the south wall of the Kitchen-garden, to within fifteen feet of the west wall of the same, at which distance from the wall it continues in a northerly direction till it comes to the high road leading to Hampton, which it crosses, and passing through a house, the property of Mr. Evans, proceeds in a straight line to an oak tree in Bushy-park, and thence to a tree on the west side of the avenue leading from Hampton-court to Teddington, up which avenue it continues nearly to the end of the park, where it leaves the town division, and joining the parish of Teddington, proceeds in an easterly direction to a tree close to the foot-path leading from Teddington-park-gate to Hampton-wick, whence it goes out of Bushy-park, and crossing a road, called Sandy-lane, passes round two pieces of land, called the Pepper-pieces, and again enters the park for a short distance; it then again leaves the park, and proceeds eastward till it reaches the river Thames, where, leaving the parish of Teddington, and rejoining that of Kingston, it continues along the centre of the river till it reaches Kingston-bridge where the boundary commenced; an isolated portion at the north western extremity of the district is bounded on the east and north by the parish of Teddington, and on the west and south by the town division of Hampton, which district is more particularly described in the accompanying plan, and is therein surrounded by a red line.

Immediately north of this point, the High Street divided into three routes shaped like the head of a trident. The left prong headed north west towards Hounslow Heath, passing the western boundary of Teddington. The central prong proceeded north towards Twickenham, passing the eastern end of Teddington High Street. The right prong stayed close to the river and eventually rejoined the central road at its junction with Teddington High Street. South of the focal point, the High Street soon turned south-west as it headed between the walls of the two Royal Parks on its way to the palace and Hampton Court Green. The road system had probably been unchanged for centuries. The first new road (Church Grove) was built in 1830 to provide access to the new church of St John the Baptist.

When St John's became the Parish Church, the authorities used the River Thames to define the eastern and southern parish boundary (see page 4) while the western border skirted the front of Hampton Court Palace and then almost exactly followed the line of Chestnut Avenue in Bushy Park. Only the northern limits lay close to an existing community and the irregular path of the boundary at this point shows how existing arrangements with the neighbouring parish of Teddington were accommodated.

*

There are no direct records of population numbers in Hampton Wick before 1800. However, it is probable that the historical population trend would broadly mirror that of London itself - which grew from 600,000 to one million over the course of the 1700's. On this basis, the population of Hampton Wick in 1700 was probably around 350.

The first national Census of 1801 shows the population of Hampton Wick itself (i.e. excluding the Palace) had grown to around 600. By 1861 this had become 2,000 and by 1891 around 2,400. The population peaked in 1951 at 3,400.

To cater for this more than five-fold increase since 1801, the infrastructure of the village underwent dramatic changes in several distinct phases. The early stages of growth took place along the existing road system. Open fields disappeared under housing and, by the end of the 1850s, many of the available roadside plots were full: cottages and tenements for the workers, substantial villa blocks for the middle class and extensive mansions with gardens to the river for the wealthy. The schools for girls and boys were built in 1837 and 1843 respectively - the latter included a public library room. Twenty-three shops and eight pubs served the population.

The next phase of development - fuelled by both the accelerating birth rate and the arrival of the railway in 1863 - required the release of more land and the provision of new roads to access it. East of the High Street, Station Road and Seymour Road were laid out in the 1860's followed by Glamorgan Road in the 1880's. West of the High Street, Vicarage Road and Cedars Road together with School Road arrived in the 1880's, followed by Warwick Road in the 1890's. By 1900, the High Street had 51 shops and seven pubs. The Local Board had built its offices on the High Street in 1884 and the *Assembly Rooms* were opened on Park Road in 1889. Both schools were expanded in the 1880's and several small private academies flourished in the village. The Roman Catholic Church opened in 1893 and the Baptist Chapel in 1905.

The start of the new century in fact saw a small temporary reduction in available housing when preparation for the arrival of the trams required a programme of demolition on the High Street, mainly of older run-down housing stock. Not only did this prompt higher quality replacement building, but also meant that the High Street itself gained a wood-block surface for the benefit of pedestrians and the increasing number of cyclists. The constraints of the river and parks surrounding the village dictated that further housing provision could only be achieved with higher density redevelopment of the existing sites. In the 1930's, some of the mansions and almost all the cottages gave way to developments like *Ingram House*, *Park Court* and *Jubilee Close*. The only new roads were Monmouth Avenue in the 1930's and Beverley Road and Woffington Close in the 1950's.

Due to the decreasing size of households, the population had actually declined to 2,400 by 1991 - the same figure as a hundred years earlier. Nevertheless, the last 50 years has still seen significant new major developments such as *Broom Park* and *Elton Close* (1960's), *Beckett's Place* (1980's), *Spinnaker Court* (1990's) and recently *Marina Place* (2010) and *Sandy Lane* (started in 2011). It is perhaps a sign of the times that most recent large-scale developments since 1980 have been on land previously used for commercial purposes.

*

As the two elements of this book's title - The **Building** *and* **Buildings** of Hampton Wick - suggests, this material falls into two parts:

- The first half recounts the history of the way in which the village has developed from 1750 to the present day. It answers the obvious questions: who owned the land; who built the roads and houses; who lived in them; how have the buildings been altered and extended over time?
- The second half is designed as a walking guide, to help those interested in going out and exploring the attraction and fascination of today's Hampton Wick buildings for themselves.

The first half has drawn on the wide range of sources that is available covering different time-frames. These include Hampton Court Manor records (1640 - 1936), Land Tax Assessment Books (1767 - 1832), Poor Rates books (1808 - 1915), Street Directories (1850 - 1940), historical maps (1650 - 1956), Census Returns (1841 - 1911), Council Planning Applications (1880 - date), Telephone Directories (1925 - 1984) and Electoral Registers (1847 - 2012) as well as English Heritage's descriptions of the 23 listed buildings in Hampton Wick.

Given that there are over 800 properties in Hampton Wick, the size of the overall task and the volume of information available have led to two pragmatic decisions for the project:

1. The material is to be split into three separate books covering different parts of the village. This table shows both the sequence in which the volumes will be published and what streets each will cover:

Volume 1 - East	Volume 2 - West	Volume 3 - Central
Lower Teddington Road	**Park Road**	**High Street**
Aspen Close Baygrove Mews Glamorgan Road Lexington Place Monmouth Avenue Normansfield Avenue Raeburn Close Seymour Road Station Road	Bennet Close Cedars Road Church Grove Park Court *Saddlers Mews* St John's Road Sandy Lane School Lane School Road Vicarage Road Vineyard Row	Barge Walk Beverley Road Bushy Park Hampton Court Road Home Park Home Park Terrace Marina Place Old Bridge Street Upper Teddington Road Warwick Road Woffington Close

2. In parallel with the books, a website has been created (see page 209) containing a page for each residential property providing, as a minimum, a list of occupants and (if built before 1911) a link to the Census returns for that property. The web page also includes links to other relevant material where available such as Estate Agent Sale Particulars, recent and historic Planning Applications and any other archive material.

The books have a common structure and, within the specific geographic area of the village covered, are self-contained. They begin with a geographic and historic overview, then give a snapshot taken around 1850 using the first accurate map and descriptions available to us, followed by a number of chapters detailing the listed and significant buildings - and their occupants - as captured in this snapshot.

Each book then traces the subsequent housing developments that took place decade by decade from the 1850's to the current day, highlighting the fascinating - and often lively - interactions between the developers and the planning authorities. Finally, there is a set of guided walks along each individual street with illustrations and a brief background of every single property on either side of the road.

The intention is that this material - viewed alongside the webpage for each property - will enable the reader to trace the origin and explore the richness of all the buildings of Hampton Wick ... brick by brick.

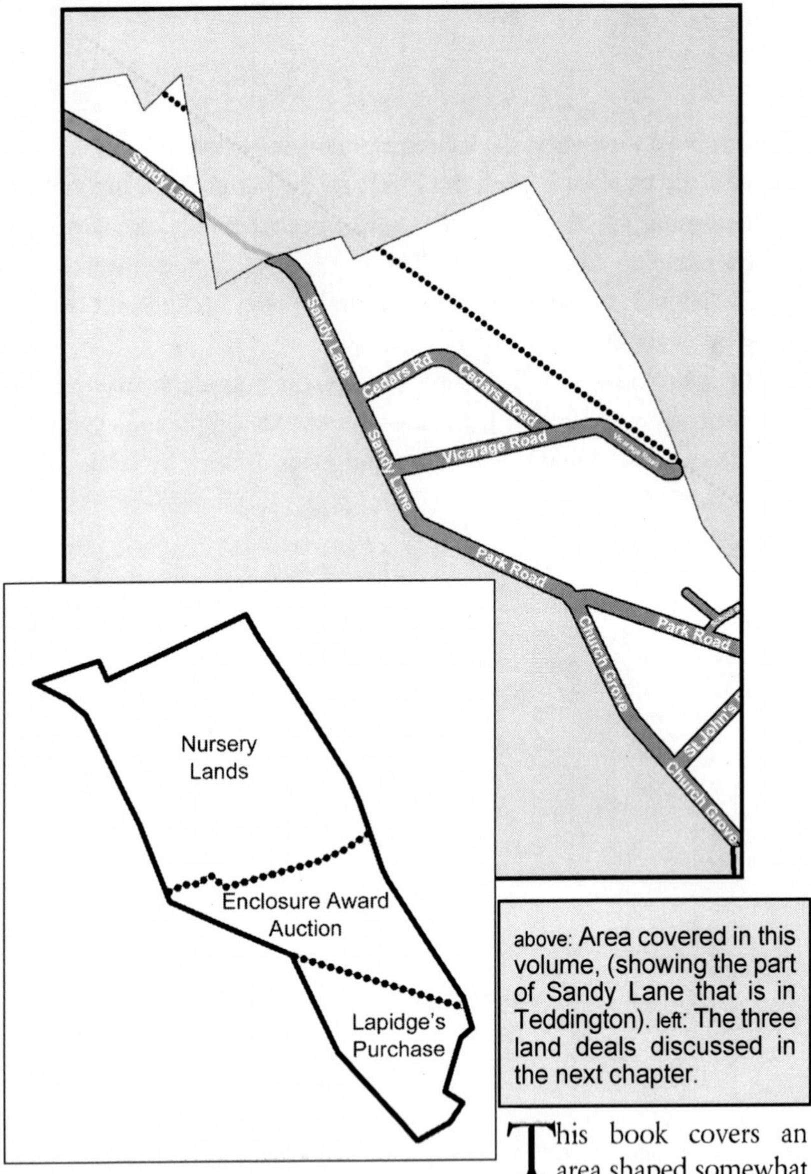

above: Area covered in this volume, (showing the part of Sandy Lane that is in Teddington). left: The three land deals discussed in the next chapter.

This book covers an area shaped somewhat like an inverted triangle with its apex resting on the corner of today's Church Grove, opposite the Old King's Head. This area is bounded on its west side by the original wall of Bushy Park and on its east by the High Street and the railway. The top is demarcated by the Parish Boundary (although as we shall see the northern limit is not quite so

Overview of Volume Two

cut-and-dried as this). The overall shape is about 1,000 metres from top to bottom and 300 metres across the top and covers some 40 acres. Originally it had just one thoroughfare across it - bisecting then skirting it - as Park Road, with its extension into Sandy Lane, set off from the High Street on its way out to Hounslow Heath.

The illustration on the page opposite shows this section of the village on Rocque's 1740 map, the earliest detailed map available. The land falls into three distinct sections: at the bottom (southern) end is a lozenge shape that was owned by a group of wealthy landowners. By 1740 part of this was built upon with houses on the High Street (which will be covered in Volume 3) but the rest is mainly shown as woodland. Although the other two sections had originally both been common land, by the time of the map only the central section marked Wick Green remained free from squatters. The northern section comprising at least 20 acres was by now privately owned and largely being used as nursery gardens. There was little habitation save for a few cottages at the southern end of Park Road reached by an alley up to what is now School Lane. There was also some isolated property (probably a farm-house and farm-workers' cottages) on the nursery grounds.

As we shall trace in this book, over time a comprehensive network of roads and houses developed. In chronological order these were: Church Grove and St John's Road (1830s), then Cedars and Vicarage Roads (mid 1880s) and finally School Road (late 1880s). Subsequent infilling was facilitated by the development of a series of cul-de-sacs: Park Court (1930s), Vineyard Row and Bennet Close (1970s), *Saddlers Mews* (1980s), and most recently, *St John's Mews* and Southcott Road (2010). However it was the ownership of each of the three sections of land described above that dictated the history and direction of all this development. Since the ownership of all three underwent significant changes during the 1820's, these land deals are a sensible point at which to start our narrative.

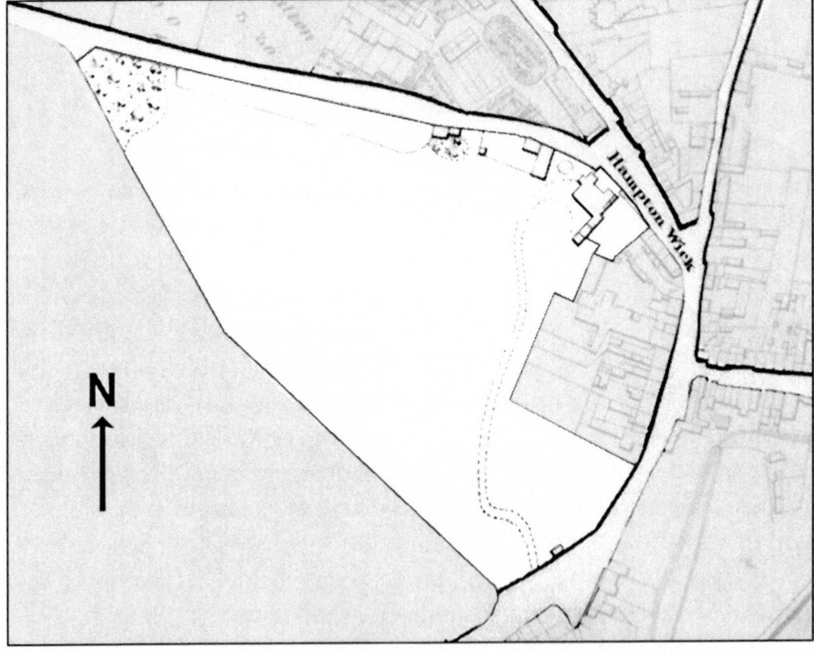

Figure 1: Hampton Wick House as it appears in the Enclosure Award map of 1828. It faced onto the High Street at St John's Place on the site now occupied by Sigma Sport. The carriage entrance was on Hampton Court Road and a winding drive led to the back of the house. At the northwest corner was an area with trees - possibly an orchard.

Edward Lapidge's purchase of this property and its land in 1826 was the basis for the subsequent developments on Church Grove, St John's Road and the southwest side of Park Road.

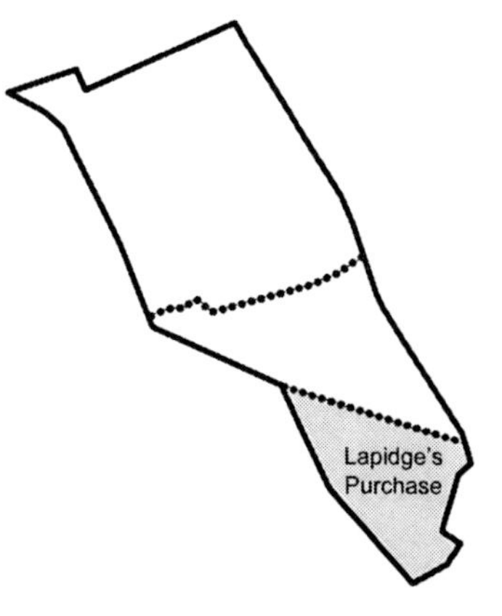

The Land Deals

1. Edward Lapidge's Purchase

The events leading up to Edward Lapidge's purchase are worth examining in some detail because they provide some fascinating insights into the people and processes involved in land-ownership in Hampton Wick during the early nineteenth century. The story begins in 1780 when Dorothy Phelp is about to marry Charles Joseph Vibert, Marquis de la Pierre, Captain of the Regiment of Cavalry of Savoy in the service of the King of Sardinia. She is a very wealthy woman in her own right being sole heiress (since the age of 3) of John Phelp who owns property in the Manors of Hampton Court, Ealing and Richmond. Before their nuptials, Charles and Dorothy prepare a Marriage Contract. The document identifies the sources of Miss Phelp's wealth and the settlement of it in great detail. It runs to 56 pages. As part of the arrangement, Dorothy passes much of her property to one Daniel Macnamara with instructions to invest money arising from sale of premises into a trust.

We next catch up with Dorothy when she is mentioned in the Court Rolls of Hampton Court Manor. The Rolls are transcripts of the proceedings of the Manor of Hampton Court relating to property and tenancy in the jurisdiction of the Manor. As well as Hampton Court itself, this also covered modern-day Hampton, Hampton Hill and Hampton Wick. The Rolls record that, at an out of court hearing on 26 November 1825, three people applied through their Attorney to surrender back to the Manor a property of which they were currently tenants. The parties were described as follows:

> *Maria Faulkner of O'Brien's Bridge in the Country of Clare in the Kingdom of Ireland Widow only child and Heiress at Law of Lucinda MacNamara of Castle Town and Ardelomy in the County of Clare in the Kingdom of Ireland Widow deceased*

Mary Bouchier of De Crespigny Terrace Camberwell in the County of Surrey Widow and Relict of John Bouchier late of Kelfruish in the County of Limerick in the Kingdom of Ireland Esquire a Major General in the Royal Irish Artillery

Margaret O'Brien of the City of Bath Widow.

Lucinda, Mary and Margaret were each daughters and heiresses of the Daniel MacNamara who had been appointed trustee for Dorothy Phelp's property portfolio. The connection further emerges in the description of the property being surrendered:

All that Customary Capital messuage or Dwellinghouse and the Appurtenances thereof called Hampton Wick House situate at Hampton Wick within the said Honor and Manor together with the Offices Coachhouse Stable Pleasure Grounds Gardens and pieces or parcels of Land thereunto belonging containing in the whole Nine Acres or thereabouts which said Messuage or Tenement and Premises were late in the occupation of Dorothy Marchioness de la Pierre and are now in the occupation of ...

Frustratingly, the clerk of the court left a gap for the name of the current occupant to be inserted but never got round to filling it in, making it difficult to be sure at this stage exactly where the property was located. We are then told that the surrender is

in consideration of Four thousand five hundred pounds paid by Edward Lapidge of Green Street Grosvenor Square in the County of Middlesex architect.

Lapidge was a local boy, born at Hampton Court on 21 June 1779. His father and grandfather had both been Head Gardener at Hampton Court Palace where Edward's Godfather - Lancelot "Capability" Brown - was another and probably best-known holder of that post. Lapidge's family moved into The Grove on Lower Teddington Road in 1796. Edward Lapidge had moved to Grosvenor Square in 1812 to set up his architectural practice. He later inherited The Grove along with several other properties at Hampton Court so he was certainly not a newcomer to real estate at the time of this current transaction. But he had a double interest in acquiring Hampton Wick House as we shall soon see.

The transfer was completed at a Court Session on 11 February 1826 with Lapidge paying £45 for the equivalent of today's Stamp Duty Land Tax. He soon returned to the Court with a request to enfranchise (i.e. purchase the freehold of) the property. The certificate noted the consideration:

> *Received the 9th Day of August 1826 from the abovenamed Edward Lapidge the Sum of four hundred and fifty six pounds fifteen shillings of money*

and contained a fuller description of the property:

> *the site thereof 7 acres, 3 roods and 25 perches (is) adjoining to and abutting on the* south-west *upon the wall of Bushy Park and on the* north-east *upon the road leading from the village of Hampton Wick to Teddington and which are more particularly described by plan thereof herein affixed.*

Although the plan is just a crude sketch in the margin of the Roll book, it is enough to find the property with certainty on the 1828 map (see Figure 1 on page 16).

There was an interesting requirement placed on the Certificate of Enfranchisement:

> *it is hereby expressly stipulated and agreed that the said Edward Lapidge his heirs and assigns shall not later than three Calendar months from the date of these presents at his and their own proper costs and charges form make and complete a good and sufficient road of the breadth of fifty feet to be forever thereafter used as for a public road or highway to extend along the* south-west *boundary of the said land and premises hereinbefore described as the same is marked out on the said plan hereto*

The first and overwhelming reason for Lapidge to acquire the property was that its position immediately next to the rest of the built-up areas of Hampton Wick assured its value as future building land. The second small yet significant reason becomes clear from a further transaction in the Court Roll a few months later recording that Edward Lapidge

> *... in consideration of the Sum of One hundred Pounds of lawful English money to him paid by the Bailiffs and Freemen of ... Kingston upon*

Thames pursuant to a contract entered into by the said Bailiffs and Freemen by virtue of an Act of Parliament ... intituled "An Act for the rebuilding of Kingston Bridge and for improving and making suitable approaches thereto" ...surrenders all that piece of Ground being twenty feet in width in the Centre and in length Two hundred and sixty feet ... for the purpose of widening the Road from the said Bridge to Hampton Court.

What the record fails to point out is that Lapidge was also the Architect and Surveyor of the "said Bridge" ...

Thus, the first of the three tracts of land passed into the hands of Edward Lapidge: an architect, local real estate owner and undoubted man of action.

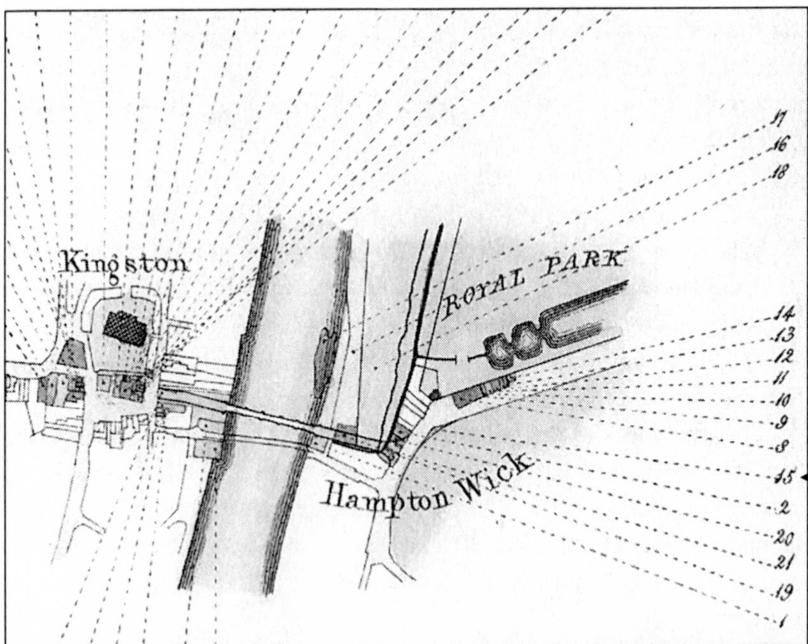

Figure 2: This fascinating sketch-map from the 1825 *"An Act for Rebuilding Kingston Bridge"* shows the land and property purchases needed for the approach roads on each bank. Item 15 (arrowed) is the parcel that Edward Lapidge, as architect of the bridge, effectively sold to himself.

Courtesy Kingston Museum and Heritage Service and Thames Pilot

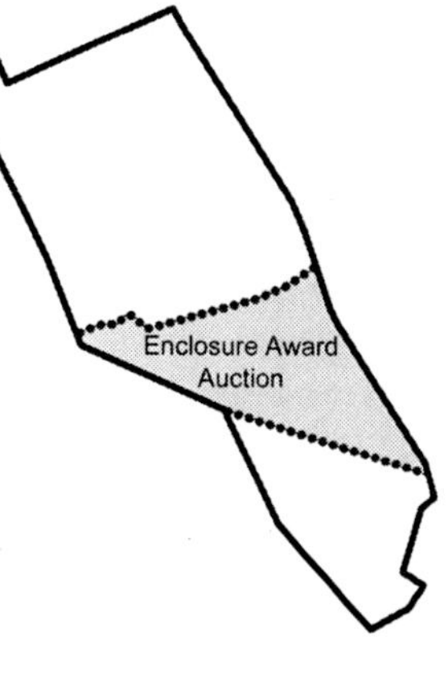

2. The Enclosure Award Auction

Just after Lapidge completed his purchase, and as a result of the 1811 Hampton Enclosure Act, a further tranche of land came up for sale. In many parts of the country, such Acts resulted in common land being enclosed and the resulting removal of traditional grazing and mowing rights caused much unrest. This did not apply to any great extent in Hampton Wick for the simple reason that the only pieces of common land remaining were the area known as Wick Green and five narrow strips on the western and northerly boundaries of the parish.

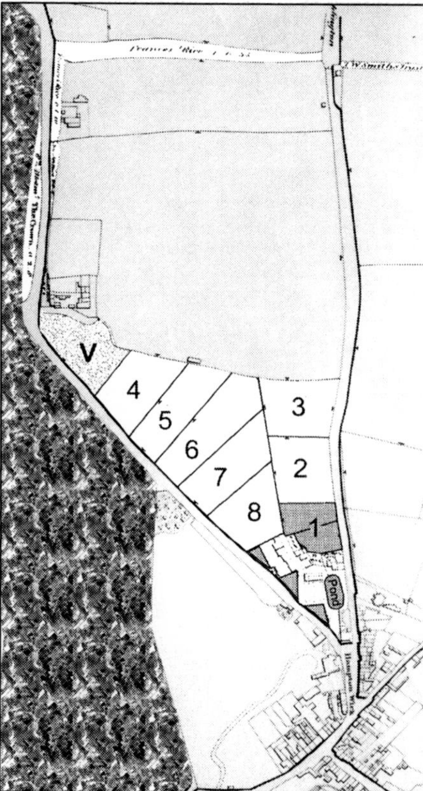

Figure 3:
Map of the land sold privately and by auction to fund the Enclosure Award. The key is shown in the table on page 22.

The strip by the park wall was allotted to The Crown and became the site on which the *Thatched House* was built (see page 33). Three of the other strips were allocated to Mrs Frances Rice who already owned the neighbouring land. Of the remaining central block, the north-west plot (marked "V" in Figure 3) was allotted to the Vicar. The remaining land was divided into 13 lots which were put up for sale with the proceeds being used to defray the costs of the Enclosure Award. Six of the lots (including the village pond) were sold privately. The map on which Figure 3 is based was drawn up in 1828 after the sales and recorded who had bought what. An accompanying document listed the successful bidders and the amount paid. Table 1 shows this list together with the

	Location	Area	Purchaser	Sum Paid
Lot 2	75-97 High St (approx)	1a. 0r. 0p	Charles Simmons of Twickenham, gent	£138
Lot 3	97A High St -3 Vicarage Road	1a. 0r.0p.	Richard Smith of H.Wick, Baker	£162
Lot 4	90 - 72 Park Road	1a. 0r.0p.	Wm. Salter Minchin of H.Wick, Gardener	£162
Lot 5	70 - 52 Park Road	1a. 0r.0p.	John Read of Kingston, Chinaman	£172
Lot 6	50 - 42 Park Road	1a. 1r.0p	Richard Collins of Hampton Wick, gent.	£352
Lot 7	40 Park Road	1a. 0r.0p.		
Lot 8	38 - 24 Park Road	0a. 3r.30p.	Wm Walton of Kingston, Bricklayer	£154

Table 1: List of lots and sum paid. Lot numbers refer to the plan in Figure 3 on page 21

corresponding current locations. The list provides an interesting insight: only William Salter Minchin was buying the land for his own use (market gardening); the others - two tradesmen, two gents (i.e. living off their own means) and a builder were buying to develop then sell or let. Their names will reappear as we plot the history of building development in later chapters.

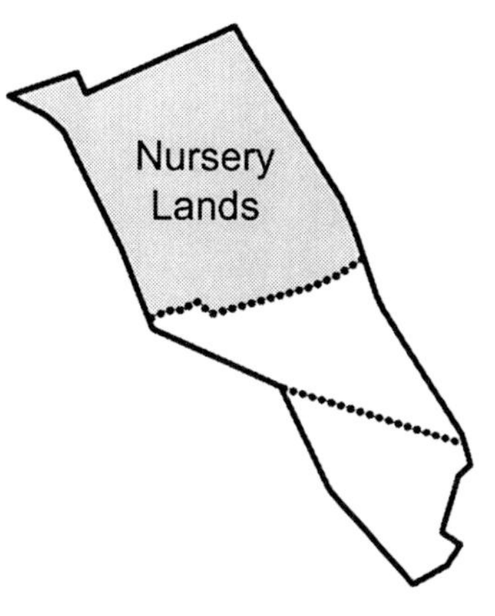

3. The Nursery Lands

The third and - at over 12 acres - largest piece of land lies at the north of the area covered by this book. For almost a century it was used as a nursery ground but the arrival in 1850 of the Hampton Court Gas Company followed a few years later by the Kingston Extension Railway changed the shape and nature of this part of the village. The arrival of the railway increased the demand for houses so, inevitably, that part of the nursery grounds that was not taken by the Gas Works was soon covered in streets and housing. The railway was carried across this area on a high embankment which - with no bridges penetrating the embankment on this stretch - effectively bisected the plot. The building developments north-east of the railway (such as Warwick Road) could only be reached from the High Street and Upper Teddington Road and so will be included along with those streets in Volume 3 of this series.

This entire area lay within the jurisdiction of the Hampton Court Manor so ownership is readily traceable through the Manor Court Rolls. They show that the Earls of Halifax were tenants of this land from around 1715 - 1742 and their story is particularly interesting. The first Earl - Charles Montagu (1661-1715) - was a poet and statesman who, as Chancellor of the Exchequer to William III, was credited with the formation of the Bank of England. In 1709 he purchased the position of Keeper of Bushy Park and was granted the personal use of Upper Lodge on condition that he rebuilt it from its then ruinous state. Montagu spent £1,000 (around £2m today) completing this task and adding a water feature and cascade - which itself has recently been restored at a cost of £780,000. Charles Montagu died suddenly in 1715 and, as a childless widower, his hereditary title died with him. However, he had taken care to ensure his estate - which included the Bushy Park property

- would pass to his nephew George Montagu. Within weeks of inheriting, George too was named Earl of Halifax, the title having been recreated for him. Confusingly, he was now also known as the First Earl of Halifax but of the new creation. The new Earl set about acquiring land in Hampton Wick (including the Nursery Ground) which he added to his large estates around the country. He also made purchases at Apps Court, Walton on Thames, East and West Molesey, Long and Thames Ditton, Chessington, Esher and Kingston upon Thames. He was obviously better at expanding his affairs than managing them for, on his death in 1739, his relatives were forced to promulgate:

> *"An Act for Vesting the Inheritance of Part of the Estate of George late Earl of Halifax deceased in Trustees for payment of his Debts, Daughters' Portions and Legacies".*

The four daughters were each to receive £10,000, presumably as a dowry. The "fire sale" of the Hampton Wick properties took place at The Court Baron held on Saturday 13th June 1741. The purchaser was John Tilson of Westminster and Watlington Park. Whilst the Court Roll does not record what he paid, we may assume it was a bargain. Tilson sublet the land to Robert Lowe for use as a nursery ground, an arrangement which continued after Tilson's son and heir sold his interest in the land to Thomas Rice of Richmond in 1792. A measure of the extent of Lowe's enterprise can be seen from a list of plants sent from his Nursery to William de Grey, first Baron Walsingham at Merton Hall, Norfolk in 1775. The shipment included 500 Spanish chestnuts, 200 horse chestnuts, 400 Italian poplars, 500 laburnums and 1,000 green hollies.

On the death of Robert Lowe (1791) his nursery operation seems to have been split into two with the northern part now being run by William Buttery and the southern part by William Salter Minchin.

When Thomas Rice died in the 1800s his widow Frances continued to manage his estate and acquired the further three strips in the 1828 Enclosure Award disposal programme (see above). Her son Richard inherited on her death around 1835. In the 1840's, outside interest in Rice's investment increased and various local speculators began to acquire "positions" in Rice's estate. From north to south, the three most important components of Rice's holdings were:

- A market garden with cottages extending over six and a half acres which, from around 1840 was operated by Alexander Brice.
- A market garden of just over five acres together with a substantial house operated by William Salter Minchin's widow Sarah.
- *The Cedars* an extensive property with over an acre of land and cottages to its north. This property appears on the earliest map of Hampton Wick (1711).

John Guy, a local solicitor and one of the most active Hampton Wick property dealers in the period 1840 - 1860, became the tenant of *The Cedars* in 1845 and proceeded to build and rent out extra cottages. Then suddenly in 1849 he is also listed as the tenant of the Brice six-acre market garden.

The following year the newly-formed Hampton Court United Gas Company acquired this land which they purchased from Richard Rice with also, presumably, some form of payment to John Guy. The rateable value of the land and buildings increased dramatically from around £16 in 1848 to £85 in 1850 and reached £150 in 1852 as the Gas Company started developing the site. Meanwhile John Guy continued as tenant of *The Cedars* until 1859 when Lionel Woodhouse took over the tenancy of the house itself. However, John Guy retained his tenancies of the land and the cottages he had constructed. Sometime soon after, Richard Rice (or possibly his executors) liquidated his holding in Hampton Wick with Lionel Woodhouse acquiring *The Cedars* together with the Salter Minchin market garden whilst all but one element of the land and property which had been tenanted by John Guy was sold to the Gas Company as land for expansion, their rateable value now topping £300.

The exception was a house which was acquired by the London and south-western Railway for its forthcoming line. In the event it was not needed and by 1867 the LSWR resold the house which was bought by one John Spink, the first - but not the last - time this developer was to be involved in a local land transaction. Lionel Woodhouse was in his mid 20's when he first rented *The Cedars.* His father had been a merchant in the East India Company and Lionel followed in his footsteps. However, although he later bought *The Cedars* and the market garden to its north, he sold up in 1879 and moved to Maple Road Surbiton, possibly finding the Hampton Court United Gas Company a less than ideal neighbour. The next owner of the Cedars Estate - as the house and the market garden were now becoming known - was a Mrs Elsmore. Around 1882 ownership passed to Thomas Henry Burroughes (see page 86), a developer whose plans for the estate, involving the creation of Vicarage and Cedars Roads and the provision of over 60 building plots, would change the geography - and the demographics - of the village forever.

*

Where the Parish Boundary crosses Sandy Lane just beyond the new Linden Homes development and disappears into Bushy Park (see page 14, that would seem to be the end of Hampton Wick and therefore the limit of this book's coverage. However the boundary reappears from the park close to the Sandy Lane Gate running almost due north and neatly bisecting the angle between Bushy Park Road and Sandy Lane by the Bushy Park Lodge Hotel. It performs two further 90 degree twists before finally and apparently irrevocably disappearing into the Park opposite the entrance of the road called *Harrowdene Gardens.* The effect is that the site of Numbers 6 - 38 Sandy Lane, and that part of *Harrowdene Gardens* facing onto Bushy Park, are part of Hampton Wick, and therefore within the scope of this book.

At first sight, it is puzzling to understand why the Hampton Wick boundary should have been drawn up thus when the parish was created in 1831. However the reality is that this part of the boundary had of course existed for many centuries previously, dividing the Manors of Hampton Court to the south and Teddington to the north, and probably respecting the edges of an ancient field system. That the boundary crosses and re-crosses the park wall arises from the fact that Henry VIII, having acquired the Manor of Teddington to add to his Manor of Hampton Court (a "gift" from Cardinal Wolsey), then expanded the park north-eastwards. This closed off the section of Park Road that had previously run straight from Hampton Wick Gate to Teddington Gate, causing the building of a new road (Sandy Lane) to skirt the extended park boundary.

For much of the seventeenth and eighteenth centuries the tenant of these two triangular areas (amounting to two acres) were the Parish authorities. The area was known as the "Pepper Pieces" probably an abbreviation of "Peppercorn Pieces" signifying payment of a nominal manorial rent. By 1830 some modest cottages had been provided to house some of the parish poor but the Parish later relinquished the land which was bought around 1870 by the Spink family of developers. These cottages had disappeared by 1880.

Even more curious is a completely detached area of Hampton Wick lying opposite the junction of Park Road and Queens Road in Teddington. This piece of land, measuring roughly 200 x 50 metres is exactly bounded by Park Road on the south and west and the Hampton/Teddington boundary on the east and north. As the only property on this land in 1831 was Bushy Park Cottage (actually a substantial Georgian mansion), it seems the occupier must have been of sufficient standing to have been considered eligible as a resident of the "remote" parish. We will soon discover their identity and the reason why they could not conceivably have been excluded from the Parish.

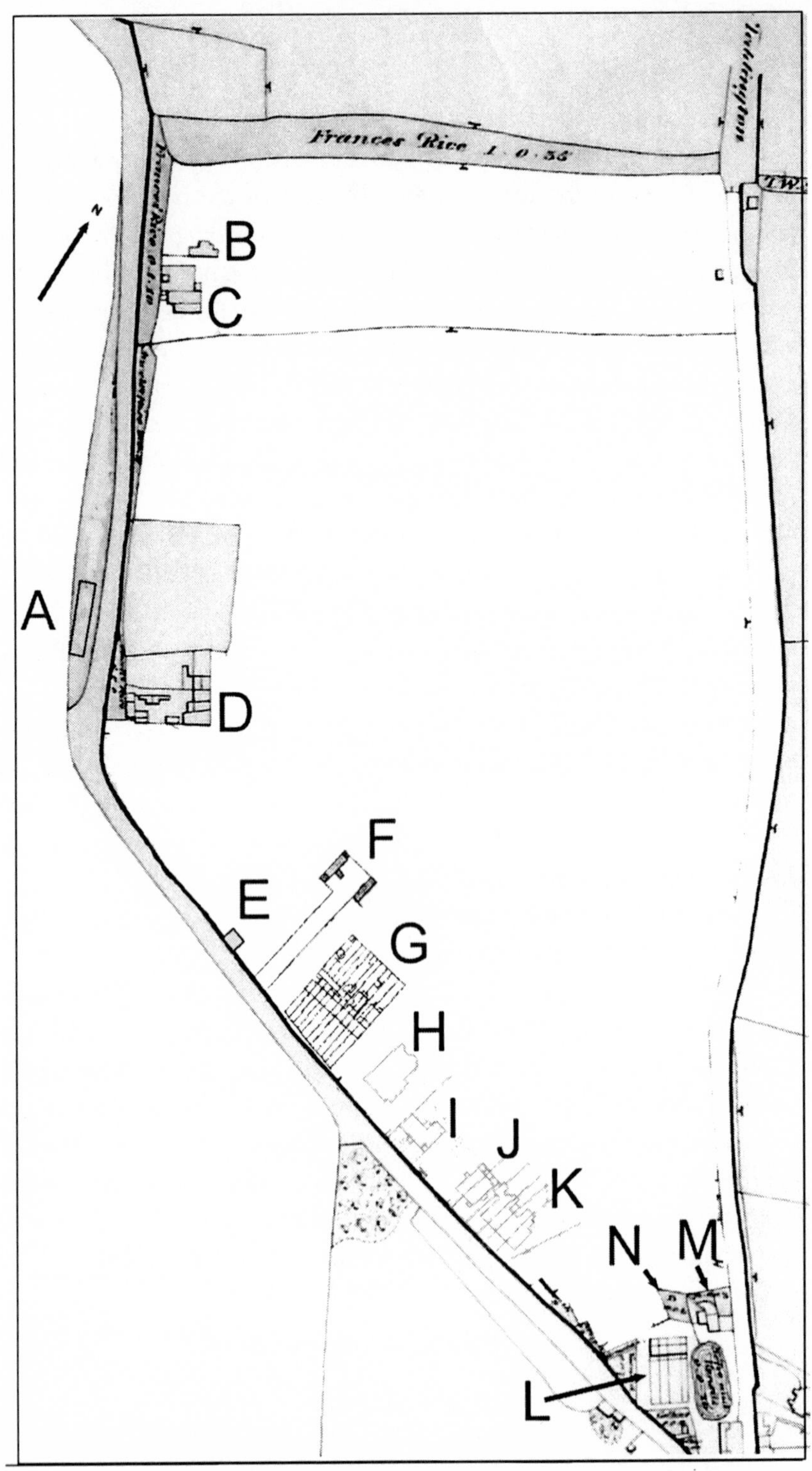
Frances Rice 1 . 0 . 35
Teddington
TW
N
A
B
C
D
E
F
G
H
I
J
K
L
M
N

Park Road in the 1830s

Photo] [J. S. Catford, Kingston.

Mr. George William Ayliffe.
Born at Hampton Wick, 1825.

George Ayliffe was born in Hampton Wick in 1825. His father was a coppersmith and his mother a clever needlewoman who marked all the royal linen belonging to King William IV and Queen Adelaide - who were then living in Bushy House - with the monogram and royal arms. George went to school, first in Hampton Wick and later in Surbiton. At the age of 14, he was apprenticed to a hairdresser at the corner of the Apple Market in Kingston. He soon opened his own hairdressing saloon near his father's brazier's forge on Hampton Wick High Street (near the White Hart). Ayliffe always took great interest in what was going on around him and, from the age of seven (the year he started school), was in the habit of keeping records of events that occurred and changes that took place in Hampton Wick. During his long life,these notes became voluminous. When, in 1914, the *Surrey Comet* asked him to provide his earliest recollections, he was able to use his notes to produce a fascinating and amazingly detailed account of his early days growing up in Hampton Wick. His description of a walk down Park Road in the 1830's provides an excellent framework for our own exploration.

Places mentioned in Ayliffe's Account:

A. *Thatched Cottage*
B. Buttery's market garden and house, replaced by Gas Works 1850
C. *Wilderness*, the residence of Mrs. Frazer, replaced by Gas Works 1850
D. Market garden of Mrs. Minchin, later known as *The Cedars*, demolished 1880 now the site of 45-47 Vicarage Road
E. Cottage occupied by Mr. Robinson, demolished 1877 now the site of 90 Park Road
F. More cottages down a garden, later known as *Garden Cottages*. Demolished 1974
G. Row of neat dwellings with front gardens these were then known as *Reeds Cottages* Now known as 60-70 Park Road
H. *Park House* 40 Park Road
I. Residence of Mr. Henry Walker then known as *Green Cottage* 38 Park Road
J. High school for young ladies, kept by Miss Slow then known as *Oak Villa* now 32-34 Park Road
K. *The Priory* 24-30 Park Road
L. Ayling-place now the site of the *Assembly Rooms* 12 Park Road
M. Barn used as a theatre now the site of 47 High Street
N. Round House or "Cage" now the site of *Sunnyside Cottage* 1 School Road

We ... start ... from the ladder-style entrance to Bushy-park, near to which is erected the monument to Timothy Bennett, who vindicated the public right of way through the park. At Thatched Cottage [A], adjoining the ladder-style, lived the Misses Bowles, very charitable ladies, who placed a stained glass window in the parish church and subscribed liberally to the Girls' School and local charities. On the opposite side of the road, a little way up Sandy-lane, was Buttery's market garden and house [B], next to which was the Wilderness [C], the residence of Mrs. Frazer, who was a fine horsewoman and very popular in the village. Then came the market garden of Mrs. Minchin [D], where occasionally resided Eliza Cook, the poetess. Next were open fields to a cottage occupied by Mr. Robinson [E]; more cottages down a garden [F], and a row of neat dwellings with front gardens [G] which reached to the boundary of Park House [H], which was then the residence of Captain George Ferriman, godfather of Mr. Ayliffe at his second baptism.*

This house was subsequently for many years occupied by Mr. Charles James Fenner, the father of a very charitable and popular Kingston lady, Mrs. John Shrubsole. Mr. Charles J. Fenner for a long time carried on a high-class school for gentlemen's sons, which was exceedingly well patronised by families of good standing, the great Sir Colin Campbell's family being amongst the pupils. Next was the residence of Mr. Henry Walker [I], a surveyor, one of the principal inhabitants of the village, and a leading spirit in promoting improvements. His family was widely known and greatly respected; one of his sons was Mr. Thomas Tindal Walker, who became Mayor of Kingston; and another was Mr. Henry Walker, whose descendants still occupy the same house. Next was a high school for young ladies [J], kept by Miss Slow, a very capable teacher, whose academy was the principal one in the neighbourhood, and was patronised by many of the leading families.

Next to this house was The Priory [K], a row of neat villas with gardens. The whole of the land opposite, from the corner of St. John's-road, was at that time open, and was used for grazing, and by the boys for cricket and

* these letters refer to the map on page 28 and key on page 29

other games. Ayling-place [L], named after its builder, occupied the site on which the Assembly-rooms now stand. Near this spot stood the barn [M] used as a theatre and visited by the Duke of Clarence when residing at Bushy House. The buildings then standing there comprised a shop at the corner and a row of cottages. Near by was the parish Round House [N] or 'Cage,' which served as a prison for casual pilferers or drunkards. The parish cage was a miserable little building standing on what was then known as the Green, and was at the back of where the Schools now stand. Here the prisoners were locked up for the night prior to being taken before the magistrates at Hampton or Twickenham the next day.

Above, top to bottom: Variety in the earliest buildings: *The Thatched House* (Cottage Orné), *The Priory* (Gothic Revival) and Reeds Cottages (modest tenement)

The Earliest Buildings

George Ayliffe described many buildings on his 1830's walk, several of which survive to this day and unsurprisingly all are either listed as Grade II by English Heritage or as Buildings of Townscape Merit by London Borough of Richmond. All were built within ten years of each other and yet are of greatly contrasting styles from Gothic Revival through Cottage Orné to modest tenement. This individualism is in marked contrast to the replication of designs characteristic of later Victorian buildings. This section covers this valuable legacy in the order in which Ayliffe mentions them, with each property having its own chapter in which the story of the building, its occupiers and the changes they made can be told in detail. One significant building not mentioned by Ayliffe but certainly in existence at the time of his walk is the *Church of St John the Baptist* which, therefore, also receives its own chapter in this section.

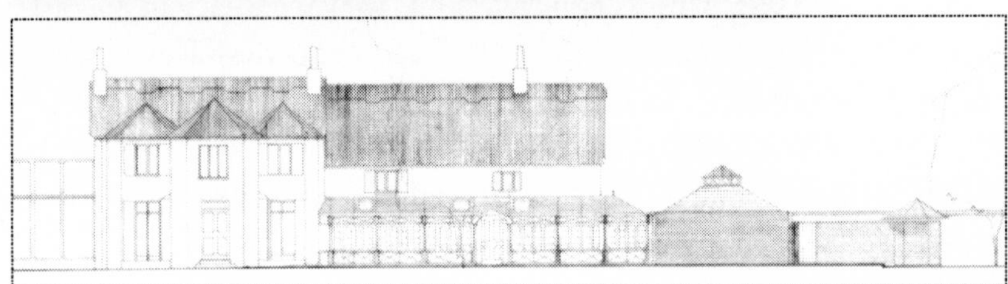

The Thatched House
1 and 3 Sandy Lane

English Heritage Grade 2 Listing (May 1983):
Late C18 or early C19. Picturesque semi-detached houses in "Cottage Orné" style. Perhaps originally one house. Each 2 storeys, 3 windows. Roughcast with thatched roofs and patterned cement chimneys. Fancy "Gothic" glazing to windows. Bushy House has double bayed front on Bushy Park and single full height projecting central bay with entrance on the road front. The *Thatched House* has porch projection on the Park front and a built out ground floor with slate roof and thatched porch on the road front. Interior not seen.

Although one of the most distinctive houses in Hampton Wick, it is not clear who built it nor who endowed it with its thatched roof and lattice windows - and whether they were the same person or different people. We do know that it was built in the 1830's and yet its style, Cottage Orné or decorated cottage, dates back to an earlier movement of "rustic" stylised cottages of the late 18th and early 19th century. The current owner, who has recently and faithfully restored the property to its former glory, explained how the refurbishment brought to light the poor quality workmanship and materials of the original structure, suggesting the possibility that the design arose from the conversion of a more conventional building possibly carried out by an unskilled owner. A sketch by local artist Lucy Millett, dated 1904, shows a view from the park of the western facade which looks almost identical in scale and appearance to the present house - so any conversion would have happened in the 19th century which narrows down the possibilities.

Ayliffe recalls "the Misses Bowles, very charitable ladies, who placed a stained glass window in the parish church and subscribed liberally to the Girls' School and local charities". They must have newly moved in at the time of Ayliffe's walk since the 1841 Census records Sophia and

Matilda Bowles as the youngest of four sisters (all spinsters) living in a house on the High Street in Teddington along with six servants. These two Bowles sisters remained at the *Thatched House* until their deaths within months of each other in 1867. There is no entry in the 1871 Census for the property and a gap in our knowledge of who lived there until 1878.

Alfred Monarch Kino was born in Russian Poland around 1846. He came to England and became a naturalised British subject in 1871 when, in the Census of that year, he is recorded as a tailor, lodging in 61 Regent Street, London. However the traditional stereotype of a poor Jewish tailor fleeing from persecution in Eastern Europe does not seem to apply here - an advert (left) shows him with his own establishments at 40 Cornhill and 87 Regent Street as being "Tailor to all the Principal Courts of Europe".

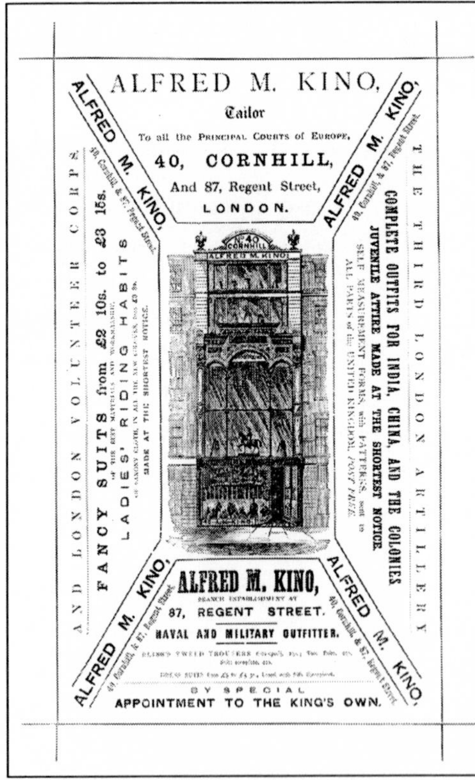

Keeping Kino as his trade name, Alfred adopted Kennard as an anglicised surname. In 1874, he married 14-year-old Eva Eskell, daughter of a Scottish-born surgeon dentist who had lived and practised in St Peter's Square in Manchester before moving to Hanover Square in 1863. By 1878, the Kennards had started a family and moved to the Thatched Cottage where four of their children were born. The 1891 Census shows Alfred Monarch Kennard (Merchant Tailor) as head of his family of five. He died of lung cancer in September of the same year and was buried in the Jewish Cemetery at Balls Pond Road, Islington. Eva remained in the *Thatched Cottage* until 1907. However, by February 1911, Eva has moved out and is living with her eldest son Alfred Dudley Kennard who is a 35-year-old surgeon living as a bachelor in a 14-room house in Bedford Square. Her daughter Ruth Nora and youngest son Cecil Gordon (an Electrical Engineer) also share the house. In 1917 Eva and daughter Ruth set sail to New York and the last we hear of Eva is in the Houston, Texas City Directory of 1926 where, as Eva Kennard, she is simply listed as "widow of Alfred".

After Eva had moved out, the house was divided and, at the time of the 1911 Census, William Holmes was living in what was now called *Thatched House* (1 Sandy Lane) whilst his son lived next door in the newly created *Thatched Cottage* (3 Sandy Lane). Both properties were listed as having six rooms. Father Holmes was the proprietor of a juvenile clothing company in which his son was also employed. Holmes junior moved away in 1918 but returned to 1 Sandy Lane on the death of his mother in 1945, remained until his own death in 1978 and was followed by his daughter Freda, who continued living there until 1996.

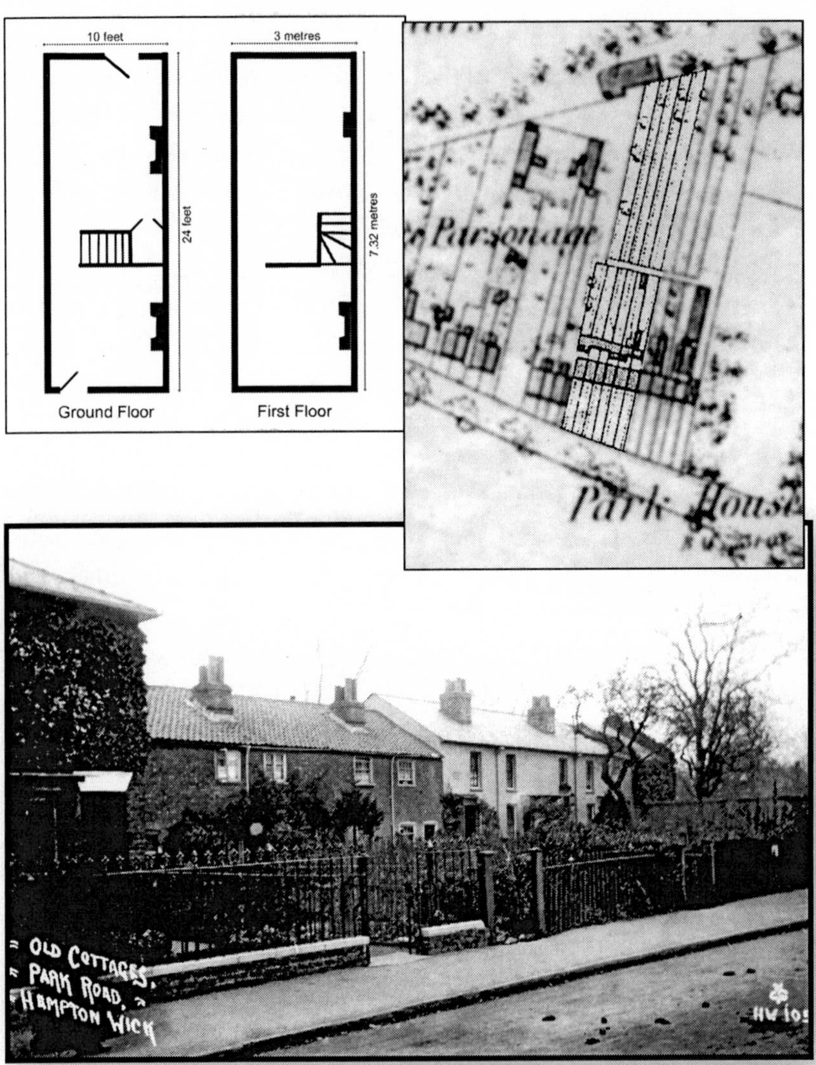

clockwise from top left: (a)The common floorplan of the cottages showing the four-rooms. (b) Excerpt from 1863 OS map showing how each cottage had its own 10-foot wide strip of land front and back (c) This c1910 postcard view shows Reeds Cottages next to the taller Park View Cottages built 20 years later.

Reeds Cottages
60-70 Park Road

The documentation relating to the 1828 auction of land (page 22) records that John Reed (written as "Read") of Kingston, a dealer in china, bought Lot 5 for £172. Within a couple of years, he had built - in Ayliffe's words - a "row of neat dwellings with front gardens". These almost certainly correspond to the present day 60-70 Park Road and were also later known as 1-6 Park Row. The cottages were 10 feet (3 metres) wide and 24 feet (7.3 metres) deep. There were two rooms arranged front and back on each of two floors. The front rooms were approximately 10 feet (3 metres) square while the back rooms were longer. The floors were connected by a small, central, single winder staircase. Total floor area was around 540 square feet (50 square metres) with a fireplace in three of the rooms. Out at the back across a small yard was a separate wash house. Unusually for such modest tenements, each cottage had its own gardens - front and back - of roughly equal depth and, although narrow, their east-west orientation and absence of large overhanging trees would have provided ideal conditions for growing produce for consumption and sale. It is, therefore, appropriate to learn from the 1841 Census that two of the tenants of Park Row are Market Gardeners (almost certainly working at Buttery's or Minchin's further up Park Road).

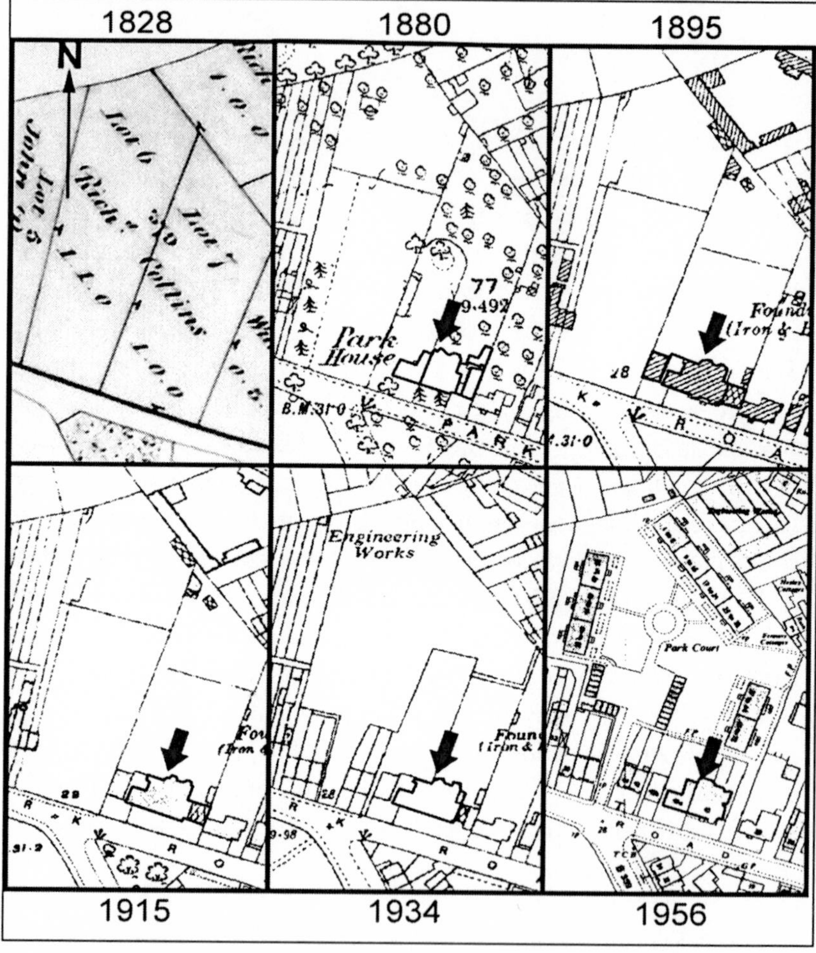

Figure 4: *Park House* and its environs from six editions of the Ordnance Survey showing the major changes that occurred between the two World Wars

Park House
40 Park Road

> **English Heritage Grade 2 Listing (June 1983):**
> Late C18/early C19 house. two-storeys. Three bays wide with altered central doorway. Yellow brick, slate roof with eaves. Very fine chinoiserie balcony at first floor level with tented canopy.

Park House, built around 1830, has seen many changes in its 180 years history. Firstly it was the location of Fenner's Academy for 40 years with, at one time, more than 40 resident pupils. For the next 40 years it was home for just two people (with their servants). In the 1920s it lost most of its lands to a variety of building projects and the property itself was split into multiple parts. In the last 20 years, it has been reintegrated and now serves as the basis of two very beautiful properties though of course sadly without the benefit of their once extensive grounds.

The property was almost certainly completed in 1830, and the builder was, as Ayliffe tells us, George Ferriman, a 45-year-old bricklayer. Given the specialist nature of the design, this was no speculative build on the part of either Ferriman or Richard Collins who had only just recently bought the land on which it was being built (see page 22) The house itself appears in the 1830 Poor Rates book (in Ferriman's name) with a relatively high rateable value - which remains almost unchanged for the next 40 years suggesting that it was immediately built to its final size rather than being created more modestly and then added to. So, the commissioner of the building was a person with both vision and access to the capital needed to realise it.

Charles James Fenner was born in 1798 in Suffolk and, whilst his father's occupation is not known, both CJ and his younger brother Zachariah (b 1808) ended up as schoolmasters with their own sizeable establishments. Fenner graduated from St John's College Cambridge around 1816. He married Sarah Harris Payne in January 1822, and their first child (Sarah Alicia Eliza) was born in Cambridge in February of the following year, suggesting Fenner had remained there after graduating - though in what capacity is not known. Charles and Sarah had no further children. Sarah Harris died in 1830 in Islington, where her brother-in-law Zachariah Fenner was later known to be running his own school and also where in 1834 he married Sarah's sister. It seems likely that the two brothers were working together to set up and run the school in Islington and that the loss of his wife caused Charles to start afresh elsewhere, leaving his daughter Sarah Alicia to live with her aunt and uncle.

Why Fenner chose Hampton Wick is unclear, but it is surely more than coincidence that when, on 20 December 1830, he married Lydia Needham Shepherd in a hall at Hampton Court (St Mary's Church Hampton was being rebuilt at the time) one of the witnesses was a Miss Mary Slow, who also just happened to be setting up a private girls school at 36 Park Road. She was 13 years his senior. Charles and Lydia moved straight into 40 Park Road and their first child, Lydia Caroline, was born the following August. Two further daughters and two sons arrived over the next six years. Meanwhile, Fenner was busy building the new school's reputation and attendance levels. His success can be measured by the 1841 Census return which records that, as well as Charles and his wife, her mother, their five children, three servants, two gardeners and a tutor living in

Park House, there were also no fewer than 20 pupils boarding at the school - all boys ranging from 8 to 17 years of age (the average was 11.7 years). How did they all fit in?

Park House was certainly a significant property and figure 4 on page 40 reveals its development over the years as shown on various historical maps. The first extract from 1828 shows Lots 6 and 7 from the land auction (page 22) amounting to around two and a half acres (one hectare) which provided the building plot. The description of the property in the 1838 Poor Rates Book refers to a "house, stable, coach-house, offices, nursery, playground and garden" and it seems quite feasible to identify all these elements within the 1880 map in figure 4 where *Park House* is specifically named. The main house has two bays facing onto the extensive back garden. The building to the west of the house is most likely the schoolhouse, corresponding to today's Number 40A Park Road. The three large windows and the relatively high ceiling in the ground floor room of that property are in keeping with the possibility of it having once been used as a classroom (and probably also refectory). It is, therefore, tempting (though speculative) to equate the ground within which the "schoolroom" stands as being the "playground" of the 1838 Poor Rates Book description and the building on the western boundary on Lot 7 would presumably be the coach house and stables. This still leaves the whole of what had been Lot 6 unused - except probably as excellent playing fields for 20 energetic boys. The triangular close over the road (lying within the junction of Church Grove and Park Road) was also acquired and turned into an orchard. One element that was probably not part of the original building, is the structure that lies on the southern boundary abutting Number 38 on the 1880 map. In 1843, the rateable value of *Park House* increased from £60 to £72 whilst that of Number 38 decreased from £50 to £45 suggesting a land transfer and a building extension.

The Fenners continued to grow the intake at the Academy to the point where the 1851 Census informs us there are now 30 pupils in residence - a 50% increase over the 10 years. The average age in the school has increased too and is now up to 13.6 years with nine pupils aged 16 or over. A later article in the *Surrey Comet* says of Fenner that he

> *"ran his school for many years with great success and as a teacher he secured his pupils much success in the Army, Navy and learned professions".*

The Census also shows that only the youngest two of the Fenner children are living at home, thus relieving the pressure on space somewhat.

By 1861, the Academy numbers - and the average age - had reduced to 21 pupils and 12.0 years possibly because all five Fenner "children" (now aged between 24 and 30 years old) are back living at home. Charles James Fenner (Sr) is now aged 63 (and Lydia his wife is 57) so is probably beginning to consider retirement. However, *Park House* is both their home and - through the Academy - their source of income. It was impossible for it to continue in both roles, so a parting of the ways was inevitable. In the event, the Fenners retained ownership but handed over the running of the school around 1867 and themselves moved to Camberwell where they looked after two young grandchildren whilst their parents were in India (the father, Algernon Shrapnel (sic) Fenner was a Civil Engineer). They finally sold *Park House* around 1881 by which time they were living in Blackheath, where they spent their last days. As a final word on the Fenners, the "lost" daughter Sara Alicia Eliza from Charles Fenner's first marriage was not, in fact, estranged from the rest of his new family. Having married John Shrubsole, a

wealthy Kingston-based banker, she eventually left half her £10m fortune to her youngest half-sibling - Algernon Shrapnel who had returned from India and was now living in retirement at Oxshott.

Park House Academy, as it became known after Fenner left, was now being run by the Reverend Thomas Fletcher, a young Doctor of Divinity. The 1871 Census gives a snapshot of how well the Fenner's "retirement pot" was performing. Pupil numbers had further declined to 14, but the average age remained around the same at 12.2 years. The decline seems to have been terminal, and the Academy closed its doors sometime in the late 1870's.

The new owner of *Park House* was Arthur Shorter, Stock Broker and Member of the London Stock Exchange. Shorter had moved to Hampton Wick from Park Street, Westminster in 1874 after the death of his first wife. He lived with his son in "*Fairlight*" on Church Grove next to the church of St John the Baptist. Shorter remarried and he and his new wife Mary lived in Number 40 Park Road with four servants. When Mary died sometime after 1901, Arthur married for a third time in 1904 and continued living in *Park House* until his death in 1917 at the age of 91. Given that so little is known about him apart from the basic Census and street directory entries, he seems to have led a very secluded, low-profile existence. In his nearly 40 years at *Park House*, Shorter made surprisingly

few changes. Admittedly he created the stable/garage block that later became 40B Park Road and he demolished the 1843 extension next to Number 38 and replaced it with a glass roofed structure. He may also have had bay windows, balcony and a porch added to the front of the house though this could well be simply that the 1895 cartographer was more thorough in his drawing than his 1880 counterpart. Most surprising is that Shorter and his household of just six retained and seemingly occupied all the estate that had once contained over 40 residents. All this was about to change.

*

After Arthur Shorter's death, the property passed into the hands of a series of developers and the house and its land were divided and sold off. First to go was the orchard on the other side of Park Road on which, by 1920, three terraced houses had been built. The developer was one Christopher Wren who had been the last landlord of the *Grove Inn* until it finally closed its doors in 1911. (The building is now known as *Navigator House.*) Wren, who himself moved into one of the houses on completion, called his creation Flemish Villas in honour of his hobby of breeding Flemish Giant rabbits.

Two years later came the purchase and development of land at the western end of the original Lot 6 where it fronted onto Park Road. A pair of semi-detached houses and a terrace of three to the same design became Numbers 42-50 Park Road. Significantly a large gap was left between Numbers 44 and 46 for reasons that will soon become apparent.

Meanwhile, *Park House* was also being divided and sold off. The main house, the schoolroom block and the garage/stable block were separated and became Numbers 40, 40A and 40B respectively. Drawings submitted in 1923 with a Planning Application showed that the separation of house and schoolroom was achieved simply by blocking up a total of six doors across four floor levels. Francis Smith now owned and occupied Number 40 where he remained until 1935. However, the once-spacious nature of *Park House* and its grounds were destined for complete and permanent transformation. In 1926, the original developers sold off almost three-quarters of the remaining *Park House* grounds for the extraction of sand and gravel. When this was completed, the Park Court Development Company took it over as the site for three blocks with a total of 72 flats to be built in the early 1930s. Entrance to the flats and their garages was via the gap left between Numbers 44 and 46, and there was another access path between Numbers 38 and 40. The result of the quarrying was that the flats had to be built around its periphery. Without any restraining order in the deeds of the original sale, one of the blocks was erected almost on the boundary with *Park House*. The almost complete loss of the back garden affected all three parts of the divided property, but the looming proximity of the end wall of the nearest block of flats most greatly compromised Number 40 itself which, at around the same time, was split into two flats. The house and coach house came into single ownership just around 1939 but remained as separate living units with the purchaser resident in the upstairs flat of the main house. When all the tenancies came up for renewal in 1964, the owner reinstated Number 40 as a single house. Numbers 40A and 40B have since been integrated as one property.

above: The elegant and intricately worked balcony surrounds on *Park House* are actually made of wood not wrought iron.

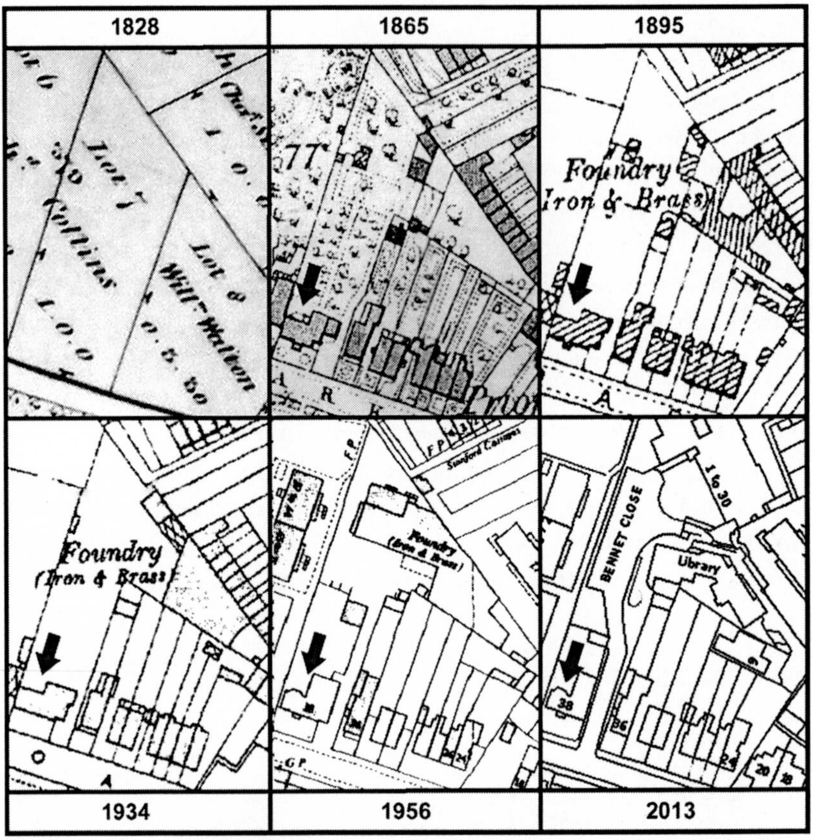

1828 | 1865 | 1895

1934 | 1956 | 2013

above:
Figure 5: details from six OS editions showing the development of Number 38 (and 36).
left: Wistaria Villa in the 1950s

Green Cottage
38 Park Road

Green Cottage was designed by Henry Walker in 1830 on land acquired from Richard Collins. That much is sure but *which* Henry Walker designed it is a matter of conjecture since both father and son lived there from the outset and both shared the same name and profession - that of surveyor/architect. Between them, they decided to place the building on the south-west corner of the plot, leaving plenty of room for expansion. The present configuration at the front of the house comprises four windows across at first floor level, a gabled roof above and internal porch below with its round arch reflected by a semi-circular fanlight above the door. The window above the porch is a bay and has a segmented arch lintel. The earliest map showing a plan of the house (in 1863 see Figure 5 opposite) suggests the original front facade was symmetrical with the gable in the centre and probably just three windows in the upper storey. Over the years, the facade appears to have expanded eastwards. It reached its peak as shown in the 1956 map, and a contemporary photograph reveals a five-bay design with the impressive main bay window seven panes high and six wide. The original position of the sill is still visible above the porch arch on today's facade, and the window retains its original top two rows of panes but the lower 30 panes have been reduced to just three. The width of the house has also been reduced to accommodate the widened entrance into Bennet Close and now has just four windows at first floor level.

The earliest map in Figure 5 suggests a formal front garden with circular beds either side of the short path to the front door. In the back garden is a pair of long herbaceous borders with a central path leading to what appears to be a formal garden feature. Beyond this lie the orchard and a glasshouse. Like *Park House*, Number 38 also owned garden ground on the south-west side of Park Road.

In 1850, following the death of his father, John Walker the younger carved out a narrow strip in the east side of the plot on which he built 36 Park Road, *Virginia Lodge* - later renamed *Compton Lodge* (see below left).

It is likely that Number 38 changed its name to the present *Wisteria Villa* at the same time. The house remained in the same family from 1830 (see The Walker Family on page 90) until Victor Moyle bought it in 1943. Moyle was the proprietor of a brass foundry - one of three in Hampton Wick at the time - which occupied the land at the back of 24-34 Park Road and which was approached through School Lane. The purchase not only put the business on his back doorstep (he had previously lived in Cambridge Road Teddington) but also gave him room to expand it into his own back garden (as seen in the 1956 map in Figure 5, page 48). The address changed from 10 School Lane to 38 Park Road, and access to the foundry was now down the gap between Numbers 38 and 36. Moyle retired in 1965 aged 65 and moved out of the area. The house and the foundry remained empty as the site had by now become part of a major redevelopment scheme in the 1970s which involved the sale of the three empty schools buildings on the High Street/School Road to a property developer in return for which the foundry site became home to the new Hampton Wick Library and Bullen Hall, a Council-run community meeting hall - named after a former Hampton Wick UDC Council Chairman who was also, ironically, another local brass foundry proprietor.

Oak Villa
32/34 Park Road

William Walton, a builder from Kingston, had bought lot 8 in the 1828 auction of Wick Green. On it, he erected two properties - *Oak Villa* and *The Priory* (see page 53) - in widely different styles. He remained the owner of both until his death around 1850 when they were sold by his executors.

Oak Villa was built around 1829 as a pair of semi-detached houses. Accommodation was a modest four-rooms each and the halls-apart configuration with the entrance doors at the side leaving the front facade just accommodating five windows, the top central window presumably split to serve each house. This window has a semi-circular fanlight-like shape which is mirrored at the top of the slight indents on the facade in which the ground floor windows are set. There seem to have been no significant changes made to the plan of the building throughout its life.

The set up was ideal for Walton's first tenant who leased both houses. Mary Slow, born in 1777 the daughter of a lawyer, opened up a girl's school in 1830, presumably using one half of the property for classrooms and living with her long-term companion in the other half. It is unlikely that this was the 53-year-old spinster's first venture as a schoolmistress and she may well have had a professional connection with her neighbour Charles Fenner for whom she stood witness at his wedding. The 1841 Census shows she had nine pupils boarding at the school, but she subsequently gave up the lease of Number 2 Park Villa in 1848. According to the 1851 Census, she had no boarders although she was still listed as a schoolmistress, now aged 74, she had possibly retired. She remained in Number 1 *Oak Villa* until her death in 1868.

above: *The Priory* was probably modelled on nearby *Strawberry Hill* (inset).
left: *The Priory* is specifically labelled in the 1863 OS Edition.

The Priory is in complete contrast to the other property built by William Walton on Lot 8 (see page 51). Whereas the former is a pair of four-room houses with a conservative external design, *The Priory*, built around 1830, is a terrace of four four-room houses but with a strikingly different appearance from any contemporary property in Hampton Wick. The inspiration for the distinctive style is not hard to find since it exists little more than a mile away at Strawberry Hill.

The Priory
24-30 Park Road

English Heritage Grade 2 Listing (May 1983):
Early to mid C19 range of 4 houses in the Gothick style. Stucco with slated roof. two-storeys, 4 windows wide overall with end bays slightly projecting and gabled; stuccoed labels over square headed windows and doors. Tudor arches over outer ground floor windows. Sashes with painted heads in the glazing bars. Castellated parapet.

When Horace Walpole created his wonderfully elegant and eccentric gothic villa with its distinctive "wedding cake" exterior complete with towers and battlements during the second half of the 18th century, he gave birth to an architectural style known as Strawberry Hill Gothic. This was adopted with great skill and sensitivity by Walton for *The Priory*. Applying the architectural style of a large mansion to a row of modest cottages could have been disastrous but Walton cleverly scaled down the features he borrowed - both in their size and scope - to create a well-proportioned and homogenous building that nevertheless has merit well beyond just being downright curious. His detailed designs for the battlements are identical to those at *Strawberry Hill House* as are the label mouldings above most of the windows and doors. His use of Tudor arch motifs over the outer two ground floor windows and in the top row of panes in all windows is from the same source. This motif is also used at the top of the central narrow indentation in the stucco. This latter feature, together with the symmetry of the facade and its projecting end bays, helps create the impression that the building was divided into two rather than four properties. The outer two of the four had more floor area by virtue of projecting further forward and back than the central units, a fact which did not go unnoticed by the local council who awarded them a higher rateable value.

St Johns Church
Hampton Wick

Church of St John the Baptist
Church Grove

English Heritage Grade 2 Listing (June 1983):
1829-30 by E Lapidge. White brick, stone dressings. Five bay nave. Aisle windows painted with 2 light, cusped, "Y" tracery. Buttresses between. West end has central octagonal bell turret with small spire and lancets. Beneath this the facade is divided into 3 bays by buttresses. The outer bays are blind, and reflect the shape of the aisle roofs, while in the centre a painted window with eccentric tracery and transom. Door beneath. Three light east window. Parapet. Roof not visible. Galleried interior.

The church of St John the Baptist was probably the first – and certainly largest – construction project of the 19th century in Hampton Wick. The story of its creation presents a snapshot of the age.

Towards the end of the 18th century, the Church of England was facing two major issues. Firstly, the growth of the population and the mobility caused by the industrial revolution meant that there were insufficient churches in the rapidly growing towns. Secondly, there was a real concern that the revolutions that had taken place in France between 1789 and 1799 could be repeated in Britain. The belief was that:

> *the influence of the Church and its religious and moral teaching was a bulwark against revolution.*

Against this background, Parliament passed the first Church Building Act in 1818 which established a body to be known as the Church Commissioners and provided them with funding equivalent to £1.5 billion with a remit to create new churches and split existing parishes where population growth warranted it. Over the next few years, the Commissioners implemented both of these in Hampton Wick.

The initial funding was used up by 1821 by which time 85 churches had been created. Therefore, when Parliament provided a second round of funding in 1824, it was on condition that the local population would also contribute to the cost of new churches.

The hamlet of Hampton Wick was served by the Church of St Mary's in Hampton town. By the 1820s, this building was in a state of dilapidation and was anyway insufficient to serve the growing population of the area. Hence, when the Church Commissioners agreed to meet the full cost of building a new church at Hampton Wick, it was on condition that the villagers paid their share (one-third) of the cost of rebuilding St Mary's Hampton.

This description of the new chapel building is taken from the Mirror of Literature, Amusement and Instruction published in 1832:

Hampton Wick is a cheerful little village in Middlesex, at the foot of Kingston Bridge. This chapel occupies a prominent position on the road lately formed through the village, having its Western front towards Bushy Park and the road leading to Hampton Court. The character of the building is the modern Gothic, forming an agreeable elevation, without any display of ornament. The building is faced with Suffolk brick and Bath stone. The interior dimensions are sixty-five feet by forty-three feet, with galleries on three sides, and a handsome recessed window over the altar-piece of the east end. The principal timbers of the roof are formed into Gothic perforated compartments, which give an addition of height to the chapel, and airy, decorative ceiling, at a small expense. The chapel is calculated to contain 800 sittings, of which 400 are free and unappropriated; and great benefit is anticipated from its erection in this populous neighbourhood, the parish

church being at the distance of 2 miles and a half from the hamlet. The architect was Mr Lapidge, who built Kingston Bridge, in the immediate vicinity. Mr Lapidge generously gave the site and enclosed one side of the ground at his own expense. The building was defrayed by a parliamentary grant from His Majesty's Church Commissioners, on an understanding with the parishioners, that the church at Hampton should, at the same time, be enlarged by the parish. The cost of the Chapel and the enclosure of the site was about £4500. The first stone was laid on 7 October, 1829, and the building was finished previous to 8 November, 1830.

Less than a year later on 13 July 1831, the London Gazette carried the announcement that the Church Commissioners had decreed that Hampton Wick should become an ecclesiastical district in its own right with the Chapel now becoming the parish church for:

the preservation and improvement of the moral habits of the persons residing therein.

The Bishop of London created the post of Permanent Curate to run the parish. The second encumbent of the post, appointed in 1834, was George Goodenough Lynn. This 25-year-old graduate of Christ's College Cambridge was born into an ecclesiastical family, his father being the Rector of Crosthwaite and his mother the daughter of the Lord Bishop of Carlisle. His uncle was the Vicar of Hampton. Rev GG Lynn not only provided the villagers with a curate of excellent academic and ecclesiastic pedigree - he also presented them with their own Parsonage House even though the parish boundary had to be stretched to include it!

In 1836, George Goodenough Lynn married the Honourable Elizabeth Lucy Byng, eldest daughter of John Byng 5th Viscount Torrington, in St George's Hanover Square. What was slightly unusual about the marriage was that Elizabeth, at 66, was well over twice George's age, being the widow of Rear Admiral Percy Fraser to whom she had been married for 30 years. The Frasers owned Bushy Park Cottage located on Park Road near Teddington Gate. When Percy died in 1827, he left the property to his wife. The Honourable Elizabeth was living at Bushy Park Cottage when the Hampton Wick parish boundary was being drawn up. The 1831 boundary definition includes:

> *an isolated portion at the north western extremity of the district is bounded on the east and north by the parish of Teddington, and on the west and south by the town division of Hampton.*

This sentence precisely defines the area of Bushy Park Cottage with its garden and land, suggesting that, even before the arrival of Rev. Lynn, there was a reason for this building to be exceptionally included within the parish. It was to be Lynn's Parsonage House for the entire 24 years of his incumbency in Hampton Wick.

By the time Lynn moved on in 1858, the Lord Chancellor (the church of St John the Baptist, like St Mary's in Hampton, was under Royal patronage) had presented Hampton Wick with its own Vicarage. This

above: The original Vicarage on Park Road

was located on Park Road directly opposite the Hampton Wick entrance to Bushy Park at Cobbler's Walk. It was an impressive building in Gothic Revival style (see opposite).

The first resident of the new Vicarage was the Rev. John Champion de Crespigny (below), who served Hampton Wick until his death in 1887. A hugely popular man, he played a major role in the development of the village both in his involvement in Church and Vestry affairs as well as the many secular bodies on which he served from Local Board to founder President of Hampton Royal Cricket Club (he was himself an excellent cricketer).

Rev. John Champion de Crespigny,
Vicar of Hampton Wick 1858-1887

He was a true utility player in the village acting as chairman of many public meetings such as the Annual Venison Dinners and Penny Readings. He also energetically championed local causes and fought Hampton Wick's corner in wider geographic disputes. Within his first few years as Vicar he had already secured the Cricket Club's tenure in Bushy Park and helped ensure that Hampton Wick had its own station when the railway arrived in 1863.

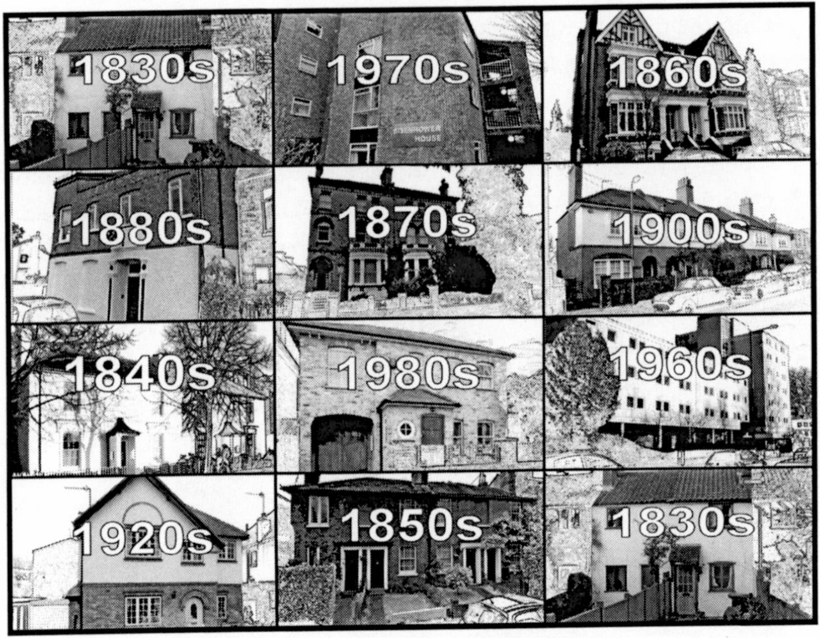

After the flurry of building in the late 1820s and early 1830s, there seems to have been almost no further new construction in Hampton Wick until 1850. The population of the village in this period grew modestly from 1,463 in 1831 through 1,614 in 1841 to 1,668 in 1851. Most of the land available for development as a result of the land deals of the 1820's had, once the initial constructions were completed, been left undeveloped. Significantly, most of Edward Lapidge's purchase of Hampton Wick House and its land (see page 17) was still available, but there would appear to have been no demand for its use for building. Even though both Church Grove and St John's Road had been laid out by 1831, it would be almost 40 years before any development started. However, the uncertainty that had prevailed in the 1830's and early 1840's was changing, and the Great Exhibition of 1851 - visited by a staggering one-third of the entire UK population - marked a burgeoning of the Nation's economic self-confidence.

Developments Decade by Decade

This section traces all the developments on the west side of Hampton Wick that took place decade by decade from 1840 to the present day. The headlines are:

1840s - first secular building on Church Grove

1850s - the almost complete development of the south side of Park Road between its junctions with Park Road and Church Grove together with modest cottages and a very large Victorian Gothic Vicarage

1860s - first developments on St John's Road

1870s - modest activity

1880s - construction of three new roads with first developments completed on each showcasing significant new construction to come

1890s - a lull in activity

1900s - great numbers of new projects undertaken especially on Cedars Road and Sandy Lane

1910s - The Great War brings building to an almost complete halt

1920s - Activity restarts from the middle of the decade

1930s - the era of purpose-built block of flats arrives in Hampton Wick as Park Court and Ingram House add over 100 new units

1940s - hostilities again halt activities

1950s - a slow pick-up

1960s - large Victorian mansions are increasingly being divided into flats or demolished. High rise concrete and steel construction arrives on Church Grove.

1970s - affordable housing schemes on Sandy Lane and the construction of Vineyard Row.

1980s and 1990s- redevelopment and infilling

2000 to date - the gasworks site becomes available

Hampton Wick Developers 1. The Reed Family

John Reed was born in 1771 quite possibly in Hampton Wick itself. He married Rebecca Temple in October 1802 in St Mary's Hampton. John Reed was a dealer in china and glass with a shop in the market place in Kingston upon Thames, above which he and Rebecca lived. He also became a property developer specialising in tenements for workers. He was certainly active by 1820 and is recorded in the 1830 Poor Rates Books as owning 15 tenements in Hampton Wick (including the six known as *Park Row Cottages*) and this total had risen to 24 by 1837. The 1841 Kingston Census also showed him as owning properties - listed simply as "Reeds Rents" - adjacent to his shop in the market place in which six households are recorded.

John and Rebecca had one child (also named John), born in 1813. By the time of the 1841 Census, John Junior was working in his father's business whilst living in *The Terrace*, Hampton Wick (on the site of what is now Kingston Bridge House) where he and his wife Alice lived for at least 20 years. The 1850 Rate Book records the Reed estate in Hampton Wick as consisting of eight houses and 28 tenements.

The 1851 Census indicated that the Reed family succession was well in hand with John and Alice's 16-year-old eldest son (John William) already working as a china and glass merchant's assistant alongside his father in the Kingston store. However there was clearly a change of heart as, ten years later, the 1861 Census reveals that, although father John is still running the china and glass shop, John William has moved out. He is now listed as a blacksmith's apprentice living with the household of his master on the High Street. In the 1871 Census, John William and his middle brother Alfred are listed at *Maude Cottage* on St John's Road and "living on income from property". The Poor Rates Books show that the Reed family still own the six *Park Row Cottages* as well as the father's property in *The Terrace* and now the sons' new property in St John's Road but nothing else in Hampton Wick so presumably the sons' income is mainly derived from grandfather's Kingston portfolio. By 1881, John William had inherited *The Terrace* and St John's Road properties and brother Alfred the *Park Row Cottages.* All this is about to change for, in 1882, John William emigrated to Vancouver, Canada and is described in the 1891 Canadian Census as a marine engineer. At that stage he still owned his inherited properties but by 1900, everything had been sold and - after 80 years - the Reed dynasty exited property development in Hampton Wick.

The 1840s

It seems the only property to be built in the western side of Hampton Wick during the 1840s was *Betley Villas* - which was also the first residential property to be built on Church Grove (at the time still known simply as the New Road). It was constructed in 1845 by James Sabine who was a master cabinet maker - though whether he did the construction work himself or employed a builder is not known. Sabine, born in 1805, was a native of Titchfield, Hampshire where his father was a baker. James married Sarah Neller from Harlington, Middlesex and the couple settled in Hampton Wick in the 1830s. The 1845 Poor Rates book showed him owning or leasing land on Sandy Lane and Park Road as well as acquiring a plot on Church Grove from Edward Lapidge.

Betley Villas

Technically what Sabine built was a pair of semi-detached houses but in reality he constructed a conventional two-storey six-room three-bay house with central door and hallway which happened to have one side wall shared with its identical neighbour. The walls were finished in stucco with the lower storey grooved to give the appearance of separate stone blocks (rusticated), the upper storey being smooth-finished and the two separated by a narrow projecting string course. The ground floor windows are framed by columns on either side, with a pediment above (a combination known as an aedicule) and the front doors are protected by external porches, whose side walls have pilasters and round arch windows, topped with tented canopy. The whole structure sits comfortably beneath a hipped and tiled roof. The modest overall height of the structure coupled with the fact that it is set slightly below pavement level gives a slightly "cottagey" appearance to the properties. Whether or not the porches are contemporary with the original construction, they certainly provide an attractive finishing touch to the very pleasing facade.

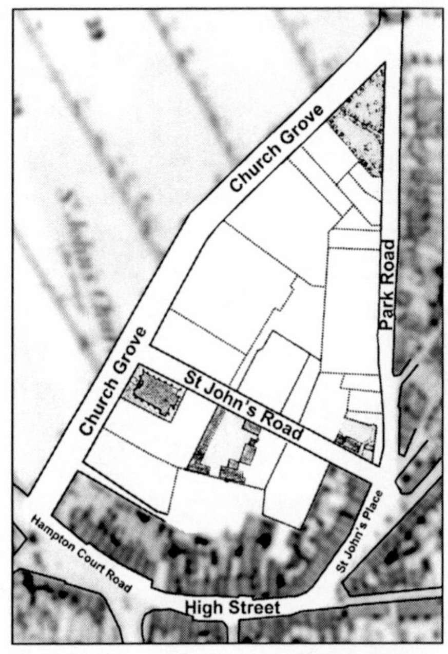

left: Lapidge's estate in 1840 showing all plots were still available. The only structures in place were the Church and the coal and corn depot on St John's Road.

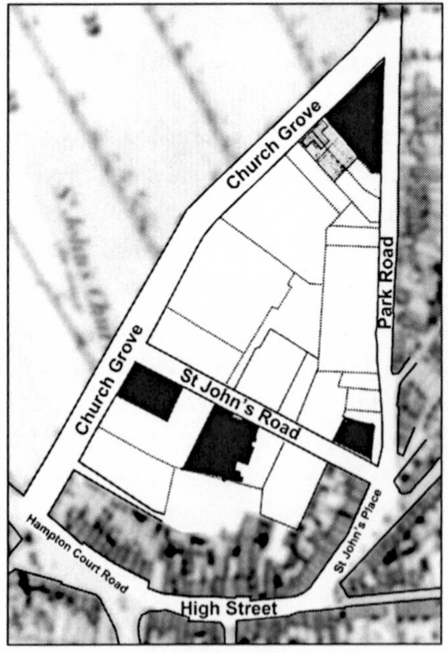

left: Lapidge's estate in 1850. Only *Betley Villas* had been added in the previous decade but all this was about to change.

The 1850's

When the pent-up demand burst the dam of inactivity there was a rapid growth of new houses in Hampton Wick. The activity was centred on three areas, two of which involved the land on the south-western side of Park Road between its junctions with St John's Road in the south and Church Grove (then still known as New Road) in the north and west. This area's use for grazing and cricket was about to end as Lapidge divided the area into a number of plots (see maps opposite) along the borders of Church Grove and Park Road and more than 20 dwellings were constructed on it over the next ten years. The third area of development was the land which had been auctioned in 1828 (see page 22) As we have seen, all the 1830s development took place in this area and, after the pause of the 1840s, further construction took place in the 1850s both of the previous-style modest cottages and arguably the village's most impressive new dwelling house. All these developments are covered below in the sequence outlined above.

*

Much of the land on the south-west side of Park Road was acquired by two families: the Wrights and the Huntingfords. The former family were painters/glaziers and the latter were builders so, given their complementary trades, it seems likely they were working as a consortium. Progress was very rapid for, whereas the 1848 Poor Rates Book listed no properties on this side of the road, the 1850 edition already had ten houses, four tenements and three cottages all liable for rates (indicating they had been completed and inhabitable). Amongst the first to be completed in 1850 was *Albion House*, Number 49, for Thomas Dale.

This initial batch also included houses for both Edward Wright and Jesse Huntingford (Number 36 *Meadow Cottage* and Number 41, whose original name is not known). Both houses were similar in style and

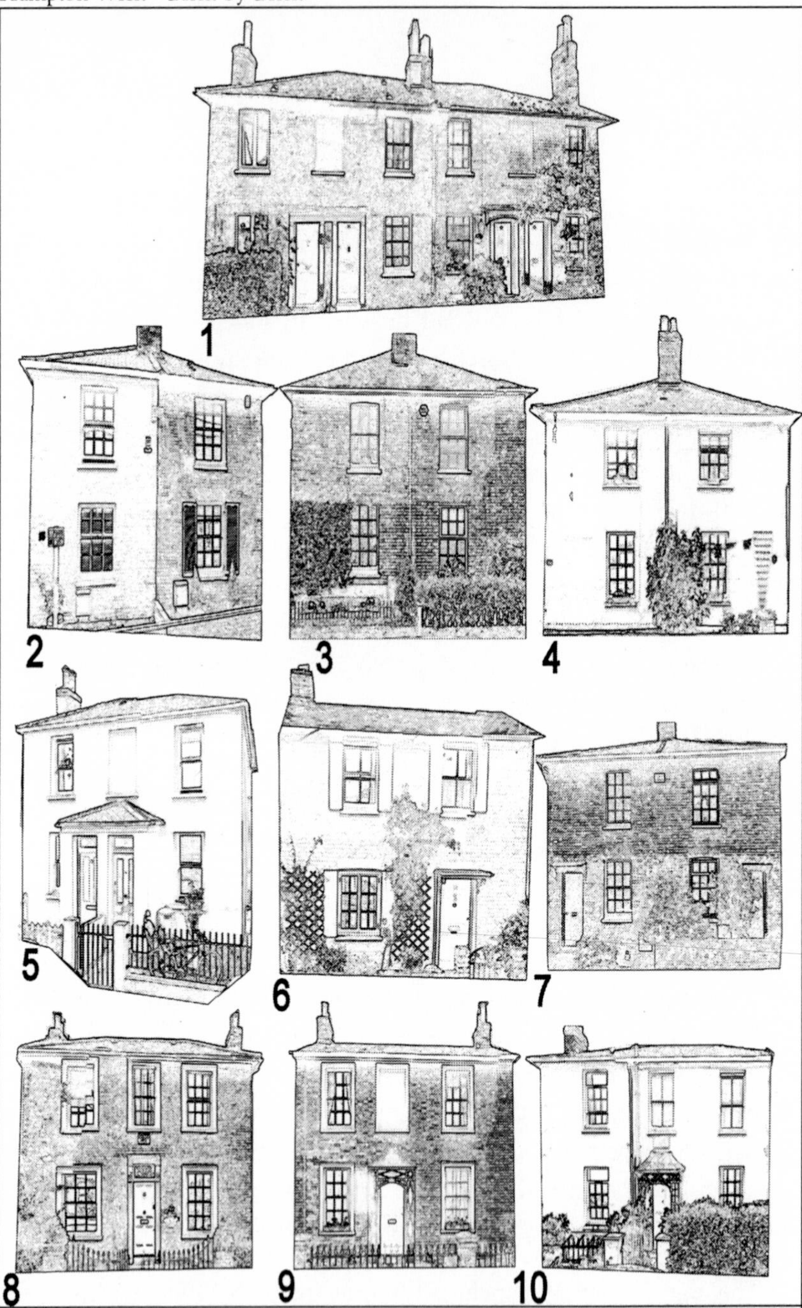

Figure 6: The 18 properties built on the southwest side of Park Road in the 1850s show distinct architectural similarities.
1. *Beaumont Cottages*
2. *Myrtle Cottages* 3. *Alpha Cottages* 4. *Cecilia Place*
5. *Clare Cottages* 6. *Ivy Cottage* 7. *Clarence Cottages*
8. *Meadow Cottage* 9. Number 41 Park Road 10. *Albion House*

designed for occupation by a single household rather than the semi-detached and terraced houses they were building for their clients. The most noticeable difference between these two houses is that the central upstairs window space on Huntingford's house is bricked up. This device was frequently used to avoid paying Window Tax which had originally been introduced in 1696 and was still in existence at the time construction commenced. From 1825, the maximum number of windows per house that were exempted from the tax was eight so, at first sight, it appears that, by bricking up the middle top window space, Huntingford was avoiding the construction of what would have been the ninth window. Huntingford's house was completed in 1850, whereas the Window Tax was repealed in 1851. It is tempting to think that Jesse was being parsimonious and was then just unlucky in his timing. However, it is far more likely that he was using the bricked-up opening as an architectural feature since he employed the same trademark on his later constructions at Beaumont Cottages (Numbers 19 - 25, built 1850) and Clare Cottages (Numbers 43/5 - built 1858).

There are great similarities between the various styles of property (see Figure 6) but, although it was common practice for builders to use architectural "pattern books", no two properties appear to be identical. Another of the 1850 crop of houses was Number 1 Park Road on its corner with St John's Road. This strategically-placed plot belonged to Robert Belchamber, a builder and part of an influential Hampton Wick family of traders and tradesmen. Robert already had a house and timber yard here which he had initially rented from Henry Walker but acquired outright in 1845. The new house had an impressive rounded corner on the junction of the two roads into which its entrance door was placed - an ideal location since Belchamber had designed his new property to be the "*Prince of Wales Beerhouse*".

*

Hampton Wick Developers 2. The Wright Family

Alfred Wright was born in Kingston in 1796. He and his wife Sarah lived in St John's Place (where the new Sigma Sport premises are now located). Alfred's occupation was painter/glazier. He was obviously a successful operator for by 1850 the Poor Rates books show he not only owned his own house and shop but also those of his three neighbours. Ten years later his total portfolio included 11 neighbouring properties on the High Street.

Alfred and Sarah had four children who all became property owners on Park Road: sons Edward and John between them built Numbers 19 - 31 whilst Alfred himself built Numbers 33 - 39 which he then passed on to his daughters Emma (*Alpha Cottages*) and Cecilia (*Cecilia Place*).

By the time Alfred died in 1901 most of his properties were owned by his grand-children.

Hampton Wick Developers 3. Jesse Huntingford

Jesse Huntingford was born 1792 in Worplesden, Surrey to a family of yeoman farmers. In 1815 he married Ann Bennet who hailed from nearby Basingstoke. The couple lived in Cove near Farnborough where the first four of their eventual 12 children were born. The family moved to Long Ditton in 1823 where they lived for ten years and had their next six children.

They arrived in Hampton Wick in 1835. The 1841 Census lists Jesse as a bricklayer. At the time, the family were living in Wick Lane (now Lower Teddington Road) in a property that was eventually demolished when the railway was built in 1863. By then, Jesse - aided by his son Alfred - had built and was now living in 3 *Cecilia Place* at 41 Park Road. Jesse also leased property (e.g. *Beaumont Cottages* 19 - 25 Park Road) from his business partner Edward Wright which he then sublet.

Jesse Huntingford died in 1878 aged 82 and his daughter and son-in-law William Lindsey continued to live in *Cecilia Place*.

The intense activity in the southern part of Park Road at the beginning of the decade was being matched by constructions taking place further up and on the other side of the road involving the land sold in the 1828 auction. John Reed added a further four cottages (*Paddock View Cottages*) alongside his previous six *Park Row Cottages* to fill his Lot 5 purchase. The westernmost part of this land amounting to three and a half roods (3,500 sq. metres) had been allotted to the church in lieu of Vicar's tithes. In the early days of the parish, the Parsonage House was provided by the incumbent himself but work began on a new Vicarage for the parish around 1855. The construction was probably the largest undertaken in the village since the construction of the church itself nearly 20 years previously. The design was high Victorian Baroque in brick and stone with steeply pitched tiled roof and prominent chimneys. The front facade was adorned with turrets and arches and the windows throughout were stone mullioned with lattice windows. The building had 11 rooms some of which were probably similar in floor area to the whole of one of the four-room cottages next door so, with appropriate sensitivity, the Vicarage building was placed on the western edge of its plot, almost as far from its more modest neighbours as possible. Soon after completion of the Vicarage, a terrace of three four-room cottages was constructed on the south-east corner of Lot 4. The land had been bought in 1828 by William Salter Minchin one of the two local Nurserymen operating on this section of Park Road. Minchin himself died in 1839, but his wife Sarah and son Thomas carried on the business. Sarah outlived her husband by 51 years and was 98 when she died.

In 1858, a further two pairs of semi-detached houses (*Alpha Cottages* and *Laurel Cottages*) were added either side of *Meadow Cottage* and by 1860 the remaining gap was filled as William Worrall constructed Numbers 3 to 7.

Even before the end of the decade, the first instance of infilling took place when William Dorey created Number 51 between *Albion House* and *Ivy Cottage*. Notwithstanding the narrow frontage, the footprint broadens out at the rear to take advantage of the odd shape of the plot. Dorey was a boot and shoe maker so he may well have had installed a shop-front facing the road.

*

Turning to the developments in Church Grove in the 1850's, it is appropriate that the first building to be completed (in 1850) was Number 4 *Fairlight* built by Edward Lapidge himself on the plot next to his own *St John the Baptist Church.* This elegant and impressive 12-room mansion with its large stone mullion windows, honey-coloured bricks and elaborate barge boards was self-evidently created to be the vicarage of the church next door. Indeed, Lapidge's first tenant was the then incumbent Rev George Goodenough Lynn though it is doubtful that he actually lived here since he already had a Parsonage House. Even more curious is the fact that another, even more impressive, official Vicarage was shortly to be constructed further along the road and Number 4's short career with the Church ended in 1856. It was subsequently leased to a succession of wealthy tenants before being converted into flats in 1929. It remained in the ownership of the Lapidge family until the lineage ended in 1948; the property reverted to being a single dwelling in 1979.

Fairlight

When Lapidge made land available along Church Grove, Henry Ryley Wilson bought a large tract on which he built a number of substantial properties. Wilson was born in Kingston in 1797 and described himself on his Marriage Licence simply as "builder". His first construction here was the two semi-detached *Victoria Villas* at Numbers 16 and 18. Ranged over three floors plus a semi-basement, each villa had eight rooms. Wilson's first tenant in Number 16 was Robert Kell, described in the 1861 Census as "fundholder and proprietor of houses". Kell's profession resulted from the fact he was married to Henrietta Rebecca Walker, daughter of Henry Walker also a local house proprietor and owner of *Virginia Lodge* on Park Road - of which Henry Ryley Wilson was the tenant. This is by no means an isolated coincidence and the fact that house owners are as happy to live in rented property as to live in a house they owned themselves is an interesting insight into the proprietorial attitudes of the age.

During 1855 Henry Ryley Wilson completed two further separate properties at Numbers 12 and 14. Only Number 14 (originally called *Suffolk Lodge*) remains and, although Number 12 was demolished as recently as 1965, no photograph has been found. From the footprints visible on the large scale maps, the two properties appear to have been similar albeit that Number 12 had twelve rooms, one more than its neighbour. *Suffolk Lodge's* design was almost exactly square in all dimensions making it essentially a cube with a hipped roof (which has a central flat section). The front facade is stepped in the centre, and the slight projection of the right half is emphasised by an oriel window on the ground floor. The entrance door was located in the middle of the side wall at the right and was accommodated within an elegant square porch up a short flight of steps with a round arch opening at the front and a tall window in the rear wall mirroring the same round arch shape. The accommodation was arranged on four floors which included a semi-basement and an attic with dormer windows.

Suffolk Lodge

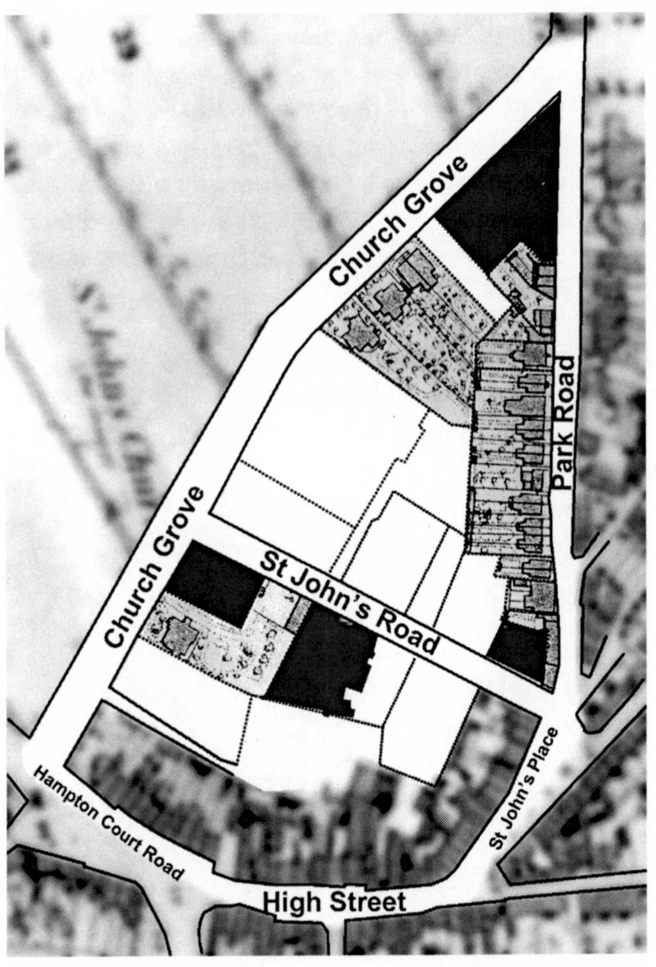

above: Lapidge's estate in 1860.
The results of the building frenzy of the 1850's can be seen. All plots on Park Road had been taken up and developed so it is not surprising that the focus would turn towards St John's Road.

The 1860s

The decade began with Henry Ryley Wilson using the considerable remaining space in his Church Grove land acquisition to build Number 10, *The Limes.* At 15 rooms this was a very large mansion indeed but, like its earlier and - at "only" 12 rooms - smaller neighbour at Number 12, *The Bays* (created in 1855), its appearance remains a mystery since no photograph taken before its demolition in the 1960s has yet been found. An idea of its scale can be gauged by its rateable value of £125 the second highest for a residential property anywhere in Hampton Wick. Meanwhile, three more cottages were being built on the Minchin's land near the Vicarage.

However, for the remainder of the decade, the focus of construction had switched to St John's Road. Although laid out in 1831 at the same time as Church Grove, the only structures in the entire length of St John's Road by 1860 were the sheds in a yard on the site of today's *St John's Mews* (Number 13) and, across the road, Robert Belchamber's builder's yard next to the *Prince of Wales Beerhouse* (Number 1 Park Road). The start of the new developments took place on that same north-west side of the road with the construction of Numbers 6/8 followed soon after by Number 10 (*Maude Cottage*) and Numbers 36/38 *Grove Cottages.* The first-mentioned was built by George Constable, a native of Hampton Wick who, like his father, was a master carpenter. It is hard to imagine that Constable would be able to derive much pride in today's version of his creation. Although created as a pair, the two halves have been converted over time using different dimensions, designs and even - on the roof - materials. The loss of symmetry and harmony has, unfortunately, deprived the two properties of much of their historic and aesthetic interest.

Better news awaits next door where *Maude Cottage* - as its fascia plate proudly states - was constructed in 1861. The developer was John William Reed of the Reed family (see page 62). The cottage was almost certainly named for Col. Sir George Ashley Maude, K.C.B. As Crown Equerry to Queen Victoria from 1859 - 1894, Maude looked after the royal stud (in Bushy Park) which, under his skilful and successful management, became famous and lucrative. We know that Maude moved into Stud House, Home Park in 1865 so it is possible that, Reed rented him the newly-built cottage and named it for him. The view of *Maude Cottage* from the pavement, with the matching entablatures over its door and ground floor window, suggests a somewhat bijou residence. The reality is that the structure is set sideways on its plot, so it is actually the side wall which is seen from the road. The front facade itself faces south-west and for its first 50 years, would have had 50 metres (including its own garden as noted - unusually - in the Rate Book) of unrestricted view down towards its nearest neighbours. A glance to your left down to the next lamp post gives an idea of the extent of the garden. The neighbouring properties, *Grove Cottages*, were being built at the same time as *Maude Cottage.* These latter were created by Henry Wheeler, who was then the proprietor of a thriving furniture and upholstery business sited next to the *(Old) Kings Head* pub on Hampton Court Road. Born in 1820 the son of a Hampton Wick carpenter, Henry first set up as a broker - a dealer in second-hand furniture - around 1850 and then added upholstering

Maude Cottage

Grove Cottages

to his activities, presumably to create extra value in the furniture he was buying in. He and his wife had four daughters and then finally a son. All were brought into the business which was being run from the family home on Hampton Court Road. Henry built *Grove Cottages* - which were just round the corner - with an eye to expanding his business. Both the 1871 and 1881 Censuses show 1 *Grove Cottages* lived in by five members of the Wheeler family (including Henry's sister Harriet as head of household) with two (sister and son) being listed as upholsterers and three (daughters) as shop assistants. Meanwhile, Henry and his wife were totally remodelling the family home converting it into an extensive and impressive building housing a furniture showroom and warehouse. The current building at 3 - 11 Hampton Court Road retains all the features created by Wheeler. By 1891 Henry and his wife had retired into 2 *Grove Cottages* and his son - and eventually - grandson took over the business, which they ran until the mid-1950s.

On the south-east side of St John's Road, the yard and sheds mentioned above were being used by John Plow Smith in conjunction with his corn and coal merchant's business on the High Street. Smith had been born in Kingston in 1813, the son of a lighterman, and set up his own business in 1850. The supply of corn and coal - to fuel both the transport and the heating systems of the day - was a natural combination since both were essential supplies that would be ordered and delivered to a household on a regular basis. With no immediate rivals in the area, Smith would have been a supplier to a significant proportion of the local community. He also served the community both as a Local Board member and as the long-standing Vicar's Churchwarden as well as being a regular supporter of social and charitable activities. As well as his yard, Smith had also owned other land in the road since the 1840s. In 1863, he started building on this to create a very imposing pair of semi-detached houses. He named them *de la Pierre Villas* in reference to the one-time owner of the land (see page 17).

The architect of the villas was Henry Walker, but both he and Smith got into deep water over failing to apply for planning permission on the building (see page 57). Whatever the faults in their bureaucratic skills, the structure they created was obviously designed to impress and it succeeds. Ranged over four floors - including a semi-basement and an attic - the scale and height of the property is emphasised by the adoption of full three-storey bay windows with the attic window set within a tall gable and the entire structure topped with steeply pitched tiled roofs and prominent chimneys. The fabric of the building is extensively adorned mainly in a neoclassical style. All windows except those in the attic are surmounted by substantial ornate white stone entablatures resting on brick and stone pilasters. Both the cornice and the capitals have modillion brackets underneath, the cornice itself being complemented by similar projecting sills supported on corbels below the windows. Each of the side-by-side front doors of the halls-together configuration is reached up its own steep flight of nine steps and is located within an open-fronted internal porch. The two openings are linked by a double-width entablature supported on three stone fluted pilasters. The whole neoclassical effect is offset by the inclusion of starkly geometric magpie work set in white rough cast in the front gables. Although completed in 1864, John Plow Smith did not move into his new house until the early 1870s when he sold his business and retired. He lived there until his 85th year and was buried in Teddington Cemetery. As the largest building in the road by far and, for many years, the only residential structure on the south-east side of the road, *de la Pierre Villas* would have stood out as a manifestation of Smith's commercial success and social standing.

De la Pierre Villas

House Building and the Byelaws

Soon after the Hampton Wick Local Board was formed in June 1863, it sought powers to require developers to submit plans and get permission from the Board before construction could begin. This was seen in some quarters as high-handed and intrusive but nevertheless the Board stuck to its intentions, and duly received approval for the necessary Byelaws from the Home Secretary, Sir George Grey, in February 1864. These were then published and distributed throughout the village. The first reported violation of the Byelaws relating to Planning Permission related to *de la Pierre Villas* and involved the developer John Plow Smith and his architect Henry Walker — both of whom were members of the nine man Board. In the following extract from the *Surrey Comet* of November 14 1864, the reporter has used great skill and tact to report the substance rather than the emotion of the discussion.

HAMPTON WICK.

LOCAL GOVERNMENT BOARD.— NOVEMBER 14.

Present: P. May, Esq., (chairman) Rev. F. de Crespigny; Messrs. Nelson, Coombes, Walker, Bransom, J. P. Smith, and Miles.

The Alleged Nuisance.—Mrs. Paice and Mr. Beauchamp attended by request of the Board, that the complaint of the former might be investigated. It appeared that the water thrown down the drain in front of complainant's house ran back again. The chairman told Mr. Beauchamp he infringed the bye-laws by running anything into the drain mentioned. On his promising to do so no more, both parties were dismissed.

HOUSE BUILDING AND THE BYE-LAWS.

The Board resumed the discussion as to the reception of the plans of two houses in course of erection by Mr. J. P. Smith, (Mr. H. Walker, architect,) and as to which at the previous meeting the surveyor had reported non-compliance with the Bye-Laws.

In answer to Mr. Nelson, the surveyor said the plans had been lodged with him about nine days before the last meeting of the Board: and before they had been inspected by the Board, building had been commenced.

The clerk read the bye-law on the subject, running thus—"Every person who shall intend to erect any new building shall give one calendar month's notice to the Local Board of such intention, by writing delivered to the local surveyor, or left at his office, and shall at the same time leave or cause to be left at the said office, details, plans, and sections of every floor of such intended building," &c.

Mr. Nelson said, seeing that two members of the Board were concerned in this matter, he thought it due to the dignity of the Board that they should offer some explanation, whereupon

Mr. Walker said when the plans were prepared they were handed to a builder to obtain a tender, and he, after keeping them six weeks, returned them, saying he was too busy. Another builder was found, and as wet weather was expected the work was begun, so that the houses might be covered in before the unfavorable weather set in. The plans were drawn up in August last, but building was not then intended.

The general opinion of the Board was that as building seemed contemplated by the fact of plans being prepared, they ought to have been laid before them, for in case the Board approved the plans, it was not binding on the owner to build.

Mr. Smith said he had spoken to the surveyor respecting the drains, and therefore considered he had let him know of the intended building. He however acknowledged there had been an oversight.

On this, after testimony from most of the members to the good materials in use, and the ornament the houses would be, the Rev. F. de Crespigny put it to the meeting whether the Board would be satisfied by the confession of Mr. Smith; and after a few remarks from the chairman as to the necessity of keeping strictly to the Bye-Laws, and the duty of the Board in carrying them out, the rev. gentleman acting on a suggestion by Mr. Nelson, moved to this effect:—that considering this was the first offence against the Bye-Laws, and the acknowledgment of Mr. Smith, the Board would not inflict any penalty, but would proceed to examine the plans. This motion, seconded by Mr. Bransom, was carried.

The surveyor then said the plans were correct, excepting that the party wall was not carried through the roof, but this alteration being consented to by the architect, that difficulty was removed. The walls too in his estimation were thick enough for the style of buildings, and the materials in use were good. A discussion then arose as to the actual height of the walls, for by a recent Act, their thickness is to be regulated accordingly; the architect having omitted to calculate the basement, which is not the method adopted by the Act. This matter was determined to be settled by the decision of the surveyor, who gave it as his opinion that the walls were strong enough for the purpose, so the plans were passed.—This course will be of great saving to the owner, for as Mr. Nelson observed, should the Bye-Laws and the Building Act have been strictly adhered to, the structure must have been pulled down and rebuilt.

The final development of the 1860's took place almost opposite *de la Pierre Villas* when Charles Bradley, a builder and carpenter who had taken over Robert Belchamber's yard near the junction with Park Road, contrived to squeeze into its corner an additional property - *Ivernia Cottage*, Number 4 which he completed in 1869. Although a modest four-room property, it was seemingly designed to showcase his skills as a builder. The use of red and yellow ('polychrome') bricks was a first for Hampton Wick as was the square bay with its hipped tiled roof (the main roof was of slate), so Bradley seemed keen to display that he was at the forefront of design as well as building techniques in the village. The V-shaped oriel window above the front door was possibly a later Edwardian (?) Addition.

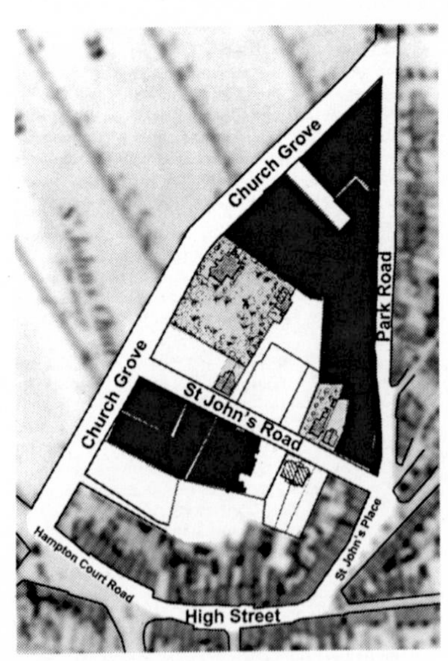

left: Lapidge's estate in 1870 with almost all plots now occupied.

The 1870s

Henry Wheeler had bought the plot on the corner of St John's Road and Church Grove from John Trigg in 1861. He had immediately built *Grove Cottages* in the north-east part of the land, but the rest of the site remained vacant. In 1873, he erected a substantial pair of semi-detached houses (Number 6 *Park View* and 8 *The Nest*) ranged over three-storeys plus a semi-basement. Each house had 11 rooms (excluding closets and bathrooms). The structure is built in yellow brick with darker brick used on the lintels of the upper two-storeys. The building is four bays wide: the outer bays contain the internal entrance porch with single windows on the two-storeys above whilst the inner bays have stuccoed canted bays surmounted with a low balcony on the ground and basement level and paired windows on the upper storeys. First-floor windows and the porch entrance each have a round arch formed of brick finished with a keystone, pediment and moulded edge all in stone. Second-storey windows have straight lintels in a mix of stone and brickwork. There are two string courses of saw-tooth brickwork bisected by a central narrow vertical recessed arch one brick wide. The porches are reached up a flight of six stone steps with a further two internal steps to door level. The side walls of the porch are perforated with a small round arch. The whole structure supports a hipped slate roof with a central flat area.

Park View/The Nest

Park View and *The Nest* were modern middle-class homes as the early tenants indicate: typically they were clerks in their mid-forties with families of two/three children and two/three servants. An interesting change of use happened around 1910 when the property was converted into a single dwelling of 22 rooms. The reason becomes clear from a glance at the 1911 Census return, which records the presence of 49 residents: one male with his wife and daughter and 46 females, all but seven being aged in their twenties. Their occupations included shop assistant (23), milliner/dressmaker/tailoress/upholsteress etc (13) and clerk (7) and all were listed as being in the drapery trade. Given that the landlord was William Henry Wheeler (who was now running the family furniture business - see page 74) it seems the building had become a hostel for his female workforce - and it had reverted to an appropriate single name: *The Nest.* Whilst the number of people involved in the manufacturing and administrative side of the business gives an impressive measure of its scale, it is hard to imagine how it could have employed 23 shop assistants in its showroom on Hampton Court Road alone. It seems possible, therefore, that Wheeler had other outlets, notably at Bentalls Kingston (founded in 1867 and operated as a drapery store before later becoming a wider department store). *The Nest* continued in its role as a hostel until 1925 when it was reconverted into two houses which were in turn each divided into three flats, this number increasing to four in the early 1940s.

In 1877 Robert Sivers (see separate article opposite) built himself an 11-room house at Number 2 Church Grove which he called *The Pines.* The building was demolished in the 1950s to make way for *Kingston Bridge House.* Even before moving in, Sivers was also engaged in another construction project at Number 90 Park Road. A house was originally built on this site by Samuel Hampton in 1810 and appears on the 1863 OS map. The footprint of the current building matches its 1863 predecessor but whether Sivers remodelled that building or replaced it with a completely new structure but based on the old foundations is unclear. Nevertheless what Sivers created - and labelled with the date 1879 and (his son's) initials - is a nine-room three bay house arranged on three floors including a semi-basement. The outer bays have wide, rectangular windows - with canted bays on the lower two-storeys. The internal porch has a round-arched opening which is matched in the window above. The whole structure is covered in white stucco and topped by a hipped and tiled roof with ornate wrought iron railings around its central deck.

Park End Lodge

Hampton Wick Developers 4. The Sivers Family

Robert Sivers senior was born in Isleworth in 1818. His father was a lighterman and Robert followed him into the occupation. By the time of the 1841 Census, the Sivers family were living in Old Bridge Street in Kingston. Robert Sivers married Hampton Wick-born Elizabeth Hill in December 1845 and the couple obviously decided on making a new start in their lives since the 1851 Census shows Robert and Elizabeth running a pub in Thames Street Kingston, a few doors along from where his father and brother continued to operate as lightermen. However, business opportunities for local barge-owners improved significantly when the Hampton Court United Gas Company was formed in 1850. Coal for the operation was brought by barge to wharves just upstream of Kingston Bridge on the Hampton Wick side from where it was transferred by horse and cart to the Gas Works on Sandy Lane. It seems the Sivers family become heavily involved in this enterprise and the 1861 Census records Robert back at his trade, living on Waterside in Kingston along with several other watermen including his brother and brother-in-law. Shortly after, Robert Sivers moved across the river to Number 5 *The Terrace* (now the site of *Kingston Bridge House*) which was just opposite York Terrace - at the foot of which the coaling wharves were located. In 1869 Robert and Elizabeth produced a son, Robert John. Robert senior made his first move into property development when he acquired a plot at the Hampton Court Road end of Church Grove on which he built Number 2 *The Pines.* The Sivers moved in on completion in 1878 but had probably already begun their next project which was to redevelop on the site of Number 90 Park Road. They again moved in on completion, name it *Park End Lodge* and proudly carved "RJS 1879" in the stucco above the door. It seems likely that Sivers may have been helped in his property schemes by William Hart, a boot manufacturer and sometime Mayor of Kingston. When Robert senior died in *Park End Lodge* in 1895, probate was granted to William Hart as well as Robert John Sivers. The same probate record confers on Sivers the distinction he would have sought - it refers to him as a "Gentleman" (defined as "a man of good social position, especially one of wealth and leisure").

Following his father's death, Robert John Sivers not only inherited the properties but also used the title "Gentleman" throughout his life. He was largely brought up in *Park End Lodge* which was well-located for his life's passion - cricket. The clubhouse of the Hampton Wick Royal Cricket Club (founded 1863) is barely more than a ball's throw away in Bushy Park. RJS played for the Wick from 1886 (when he was 17) until 1921. During his career he scored over 20,000 runs which included 35 centuries and he topped the Club's batting averages on 12 occasions. In 1897 he married Ethel Amelia Hart daughter of William Hart and the newly-weds move into *Newlyn* 70 Cedars Road which they had bought off the drawing board. It was here that their two sons were born. Twelve years later they moved into *Park Cottage* at 27 Lower Teddington Road, a house that had been owned by Ethel's father since at least 1890. The couple remained here for the rest of their lives. Although they both might be said to have been born with a silver spoon in their mouths, tragedy visited the couple when their eldest son Cecil Howard was killed in the First World War in France at the age of 18 - just three months before the cease-fire.

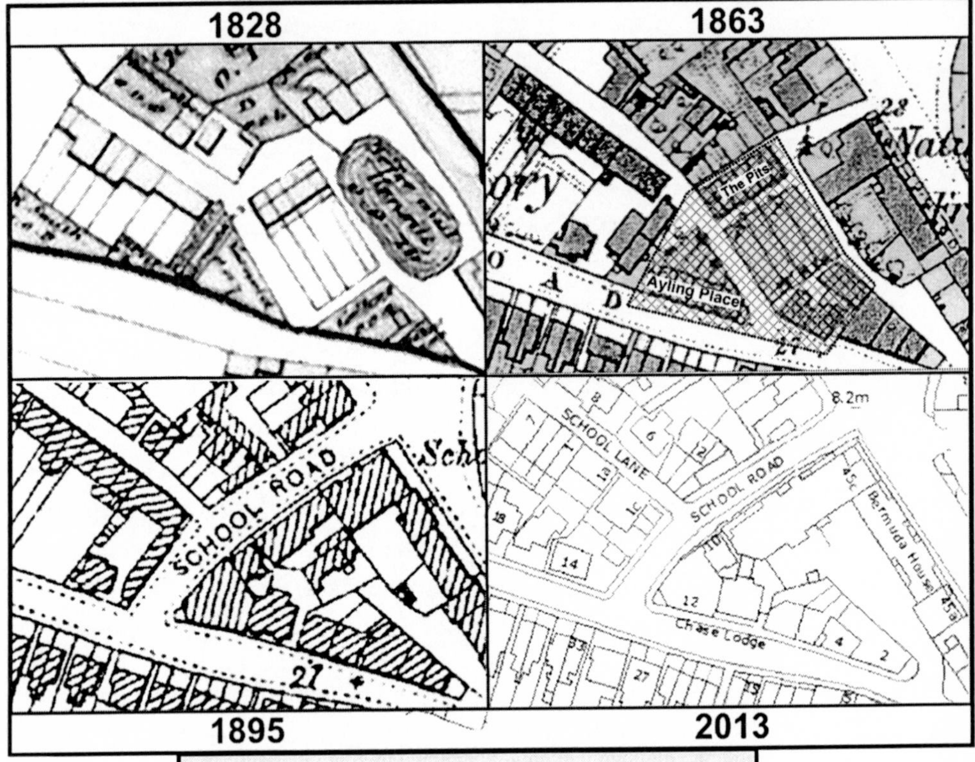

Figure 7: The School Road area through the years

The 1880s

This was a decade of great change on the west of the village brought about by the construction of three new roads. School Road ran from opposite Seymour Road across to Park Road. It was part of a more complex and controversial project that involved compulsory purchases and slum clearance, as well as new school and council office buildings. Vicarage and Cedars Roads were designed to provide access to the proposed building plots on the Cedars Estate (see page {Ref}). Both schemes had been independently mooted more than 20 years previously and - by coincidence - both finally came to fruition in the same year: 1885.

The Making of School Road

Previous sections of this book have described the rapid increase in new residences in this part of the village which may be considered to be at the "genteel" end of the market. Even the modest cottages on Park Road created by John Reed and others in the 1830s were constructed of brick and had their own closets across a yard at the back. However, there also existed a more basic class of dwelling in the form of wooden back-to-back houses. These had shared water pumps and closets feeding into a cesspool - often all located close to each other. In this period the risk of cholera outbreaks caused through the contamination of water by sewage was not understood and social pressure was on eliminating the "miasma" (bad air) itself which was seen to be both unhealthy and making living in such close communities so unpleasant. Many of these wretched houses were sited near the village pond. Ayliffe had referred in the 1830s to:

> *... a large open pond and ditch into which all the undesirable refuse of the village was deposited. On three sides of the pond were cottages ...*

and the 1828 map (see Figure 7 page 82) clearly shows such a row of cottages west of the pond. These were known as *The Pits* - though probably in reference to the pond (*pytt* is Old English for a pool) rather than the derogatory word in present use (whose origin postdates these cottages by at least a century). The pond itself was filled in during the 1840s to provide the site for the village schools, but further low-quality housing had meanwhile been added particularly at *Ayling Place* to the south-west of *The Pits* (see 1863 section of Figure 7 on page 82).

Within three months of its formation in June 1863, the Local Board was on the case:

> *Mr Nelson premising that the improvement of the village was an especial function of the board, dwelt upon the desirability of getting rid of certain houses, by making a road ... to come out by Mr Miles' house [Number 31 Park Road]. He wished that the Surveyor should be instructed to inquire of the owners of the property at what price they could be purchased by the Board. ... In case of this idea being carried out, the Board would have building frontage to let, so as to make it a remunerative operation, and the requisite money could be borrowed and payment spread over 30 years. Mr. Miles spoke of the locality in question being a sink of iniquity, and that it was most desirable to get rid of the houses. The inquiry was agreed to.*
>
> Local Board Meeting Monday 5th October 1863

However, such far-sighted schemes were deemed too radical by the local ratepayers (who mainly objected to the principle of burdening the next generation with debt), and it was almost 20 years before the problem was finally tackled. By the early 1880s the motivation was more than just sanitary: the growth of the village had led to overcrowding in the schools and the central authority threatened to withdraw the grant unless the premises were significantly enlarged. At the same time, the Local Board had ambitions to create a permanent base for their activities.

A comprehensive scheme was devised to redevelop the whole triangular area which is nowadays encompassed by School Road, Park Road and the High Street. Mr Nelson's original proposal was finally adopted on 5 May 1884 and he, now as chairman of the Local Board, was resolute in its implementation. Despite significant continuing local opposition, the project was duly funded with a loan of £1,600 repayable over 30 years at 4% interest and 16 properties were acquired and demolished. The only buildings that remained were *The Foresters*, the corner shop (now Number 2 and 4 Park Road) and the original schools, though the latter were extended along both the High Street and especially down the newly-constructed School Road. The impressive Council Offices (recently listed as a Grade 2 building by English Heritage) were constructed on the High Street between the boys' school extension and The Foresters whilst extensive new buildings on the south-east side of School Road provided the vital extra accommodation for the girls' and infants' schools as well as a residence for the schoolmistress. As originally promised, the Board was able to recoup some of the expense by selling off the plots on which the demolished property had stood. Nelson availed himself by purchasing the land on which he built Numbers 6 and 8 Park Road as well as the corner plot at the junction of School Road and the High Street on which he built a large shop and house (Number 47 High Street, described in Volume 3). On the diametrically opposite corner, on the site of *Ayling Place*, a set of Assembly Rooms were built. These provided a public meeting space which, being free of connections with either alcohol or religion, proved immediately popular with the young of both genders. The house next door (Number 10 School Road) was constructed as staff accommodation and Census returns show its occupant as a coffee tavern keeper (1891) and dancing teacher (1901) providing an insight into the use of the new facilities.

The final vacant plots were taken up by *Sunnyside* (Number 1 School Road) and *Mayfield* (Number 10 Park Road). The new infants' school blocked the first part of the passage that had previously run from Park

Road through to *The Pits* (now demolished) and beyond to *Newman's Cottages.* The remainder of the passage was now accessible via School Road and renamed School Lane. By the end of the 1880s, all new developments were complete and this area remained almost unchanged for the next 80 years.

Hampton Wick Developers 5. Thomas Henry Burroughes

Thomas Henry Burroughes was born 1834, the son of Reverend Jeremiah Burroughes and the fourth of six children. His father was the Rector of Burlingham St Andrew's with St Edmund's, Norfolk from 1819 until his death in 1872, an amazing 53 years. His estate was worth £17m.

Thomas went to Harrow and in 1852 was admitted to Trinity Cambridge. His first wife was the Honourable Edith Galfrida Powys. They married in 1858 in her local church at Oundle, Northants - she being the third daughter of Thomas Atherton Powys, Lord Lilford, 3rd Baron Lilford. Thomas and Edith lived at Ketton near Stamford, Lincolnshire and had three children together before she died in 1864, presumably in childbirth. In June 1869 he married Susan Helen Watts-Russell, daughter of another wealthy Oundle-based family (a family of six living in Biggin Hall with a retinue of 14 servants) with whom he had five children. Thomas and his new wife were still living in Ketton at the time of the 1871 Census where he was recorded as being a Land Agent. By the 1881 Census they had moved to London and he was listed as being a Member of the Institute of Surveyors. The couple by now had four children and were living at 16 Lower Berkeley Street with eight servants. This coincided with the start of his Cedars Estate undertaking in Hampton Wick. In the 1901 Census, he is again listed as a Land Surveyor still living in Berkeley Street; and still had eight servants. By 1911 the Burroughes had downsized to a fourteen room terrace in Thurloe Square, Kensington ... and to just six servants. Susan died at Ketton in 1915. Thomas went back to his birth place in Norfolk where he died in 1924 aged 90, leaving an estate valued at around £12m.

The Cedars Estate

The first suggestion for creating what is now known as Vicarage Road was reported at the meeting of the Local Board on 4 June 1866:

> *Mr Nelson, after pointing out the advantage which a new road through Mrs Minchin's property, from a point near the railway arch by the station, coming out by the Parsonage, opposite the Park gates, would afford, moved that a deputation be appointed to wait on the L. & S. W. R. Company, to endeavour to forward the making of such a road. It would be of much service to the Company, as when the extension to Wimbledon was complete, they would be enabled still more to service the traffic caused by the numbers who visited the park, and the passengers would have but a short distance to walk.*

The Company did not take up the proposal, but the logic in favour of constructing the new road was undeniable. However it was not until the early 1880s that the idea re-emerged when the following announcement appeared in the *Surrey Comet* for 10 February 1883:

> **THE CEDARS ESTATE - This freehold estate, the property of T.H. Burroughes Esq., lying between Bushey-park-lane (Sandy Lane) and the railway, is being rapidly developed for building purposes. It consists of about 12 acres, the land being that formerly attached to the residence known as the Cedars, and the market garden ground for many years in the occupation of Mr Minchin. The old residence has been pulled down, but the cottage and outbuildings adjoining remain for the present. Two new 40 ft roads are being made, the first of which commences opposite Bushey-park-cottage, near the entrance to Bushey-park, and joins the Upper Teddington Road opposite the railway station. The second road also commences about 100 yards beyond Bushy-park-cottage. After running some distance into the estate, it continues parallel with the railway**

and forms a junction with the first mentioned road a short distance from the railway bridge. The land, we are informed, is to be divided into 62 plots, and only first-class residences of not less than £700 in value are to be erected upon it.

Thomas Henry Burroughes (see page 86) had just bought the Cedars Estate and wasted no time in starting development. The roads were completed by October 1883 and immediately dedicated to the public - which thereby obliged the Local Board to maintain them at public expense. The developer also requested that the roads be known as Wolsey Road and Cedars Road. The Board changed the former to Vicarage Road on the pretext that there was already a Wolsey Road in Teddington (now known as the Causeway) but really to assert their authority since, if they were to be paying for the maintenance of the roads, they felt they had the right to name them. However, as a compromise, they agreed to the proposed name of Cedars Road. In line with the announcement, the land was divided into 62 plots each with 40ft frontage. The intent was to build all houses to essentially the same design. The architect was Franc Sadleir Brereton FRIBA, the 45-year-old son of a large Irish landowner (and father of Frederick Sadleir Brereton, a prolific author of adventure books for boys based on Frederick's personal experiences in both the Boer and, later, First World Wars). Planning permission for the initial group of houses was granted in December 1883, and the first of these was occupied by early 1885.

By the end of the decade, seven houses had been built: Numbers 35, 41-47 Vicarage Road and Numbers 1 and 3 Cedars Road. Five houses were built to the same plan each with a total of 11 rooms: eight ranged over two floors in the main body of the building and a further three in three-storey servants' extension at the back. Externally the walls are constructed of yellow brick with contrasting red brick used to highlight the windows and internal porch. Ornamental terracotta is featured both on the string course and the frieze board below the gable edges. Two larger versions of this design were built on corner plots - *Park Gate* Number 47 Vicarage Road at the junction with Sandy Lane with 13 rooms and *Carlogas* Number 1 Cedars Road with 15 rooms. A distinctive feature present on all seven properties was the insertion of three round-arched blind windows in the centre of the gable. Burroughes promised "first-class residences" and this first phase certainly delivered.

Holly Lodge, 41 Vicarage Road

Footnote: A Local Board meeting in July 1884, in expressing satisfaction at the quality of the houses under construction, went on to approve a planning application to establish *The Cedars Works*, a small-scale industrial estate at 1-3 Vicarage Road which is still in existence. Amongst its earliest tenants was the New London Suburban Omnibus Company which set up a production line to convert horse buses by transplanting the superstructure from its frame and cartwheels and bonding it onto a motorised chassis (see page 198).

Hampton Wick Developers 6. The Walker Family

One of the oldest families of property developers in Hampton Wick, the Walkers were active for more than 150 years. Thomas Walker (b 1749) was a carpenter who we know was active in Hampton Wick. There are records of him having paid stamp duty on new apprentices in 1769, 1787 and 1799 and he is listed as a voter in the 1802 Register of Electors on the strength of being a resident of Hampton Wick and owning a freehold property in Hampton. His son Henry was born in 1770 and qualified as a "surveyor" - a profession then synonymous with that of an architect. Henry and his wife Martha had three children, all of whom became property developers. First-born Henry followed exactly in his father footsteps as a surveyor; Thomas Tindal became a prominent builder in Kingston and was mayor of the town in 1862. The third child Henrietta Rebecca married Robert Kell who was himself a developer and between them they built *Victoria Villas* on Church Grove where they lived for more than 30 years. All three children lived long lives and came together again towards the end: Thomas Tindal retired from his public and business life in Kingston in 1879 aged 80 and came to live in *Compton Lodge* (36 Park Road) which had been built and was still owned by his older brother Henry, who meanwhile had been living next door in the family home in Number 38. Henry died in 1882 at the age of 86. When Henrietta Rebecca was widowed in 1886, brother Thomas moved into Number 38 whilst she replaced him in Number 36. Thomas died in 1893 (aged 94) and Henrietta in 1898 (aged 88) but there was still a further generation to inherit the house and property portfolio. Henry junior and his wife Sarah Ann had had a daughter (Sarah) Helen in 1853. Helen not only played the traditional Victorian role of an only daughter in acting as carer for her aged parents but also first helped her father with, and later took over management of, the extensive property portfolio. Following the death of her parents, Helen married Robert Farthing, son of a Somerset farmer and, when Uncle Thomas died in 1893, they moved into 40 Park Road where Robert lived until his death in 1940 (Helen having died in 1915).

The 1890s

Cedars Estate

Ownership of the Cedars Estate had by now changed hands and, by the beginning of the new decade, the development strategy had changed too. Given that only seven of the potential 62 similar Brereton-designed houses had so far been built, W R Woods - the new owner - opened up the estate to other developers. He also abandoned the restrictions on appearance and minimum value of houses and allowed plots to be subdivided so that semi-detached properties became the predominant design. Such was the success of this change of direction that 41 properties had been built by the end of the decade.

The first three of these were at Numbers 48 and 50/52 Cedars Road and had been completed by 1890. The design of Number 48 (*Eavescote* - picture on page 131) is something of a one-off for this part of the estate being a tall three-storey detached structure built in a pale cream-coloured brick and with a steeply-pitched gabled roof and a side dormer (which may be a later addition). A gothic arched window in the gable-end adds to the overall impression of height in the structure and its position on a corner plot (which it only half occupies) again makes it stand out. The developer was John George Pick.

Meanwhile, next door, James Arnold was building *Ivydene* and *Thornbury* (Numbers 50/52 Cedars Road - picture on page 131) which was the first pair of semi-detached houses in the Cedars Estate. Each property had seven-rooms. Unusually each house has just a single bay: a large single-storey canted bay window with hipped roof is placed in the centre of the facade with a joined pair of windows centrally aligned above. The halls-apart configuration has the main entrance door placed in the side wall sheltered by a hip-roof wooden porch cantilevered from the wall and supported on brackets. The house is largely in yellow brick with red brick used to add geometric highlights around the windows and corners. Stone is used for the lintels, sills and jambs for the front windows with distinctive ogee-shape mouldings on the lintels. The main structure is covered with a hipped pyramid roof whilst the large back extension has a shared gable roof.

The largest single development was undertaken by John Imray on a set of five adjacent plots on the north-east side of Cedars Road, opposite *Rudder Grange.* Here he constructed *Cedar Villas*, a set of ten semi-detached houses comprising Numbers 20-36 which became occupied from 1892 onwards (see picture below). Each pair of houses comprised a four bay structure with a halls-together configuration. Every house has a wide canted bay on the ground floor consisting of four panes, where each pane has a four-paned top-hung small casement window above. The two first-floor windows are each two-paned with the same small casements above each. A pair of prominent gables with magpie work project from the central hipped roof whilst the rear extensions are covered with a single gable roof. A design feature which had become newly-fashionable when *Cedar Villas* was being built was the use of a single skillion roof, hipped at each end, which covers the bays of both houses and provides shelter for their external porches. The

long run of roof is supported by a central wooden pillar with brackets which neatly finishes this attractive construction.

A very similar design was next used on the two pairs of semi-detached houses Numbers 12/14 and 16/18 Cedars Road (picture on page 127). However, the primary difference was that these were eight (as opposed to six) room residences achieved by inserting a third storey in the central part of the house. To avoid dominating their neighbours with excessive height, the architect made use of a mansard roof configuration. These properties were completed in 1895.

In the same year, a pair of detached six-roomed houses - Numbers 2 and 4 Cedars Road (picture on page 127) - was built on a single plot at the eastern side of the junction with Vicarage Road. The developer was Hezekiah Newman who, despite describing himself simply as a dairyman, owned a considerable amount of property elsewhere in the village including a row of 12 cottages (known as *Newmans Cottages*) off the High Street. These new houses were his first foray into property for the middle class market and were built on land adjacent to another plot he owned on Vicarage Road. The designs were simple and conventional, but the use of roughcast on the upper storey and hung tiles on the gable ends reflected an arts and craft fashion that emerged during the later Victorian period.

The OS map that was published in 1895 (see left) provides an interesting snapshot of developments on the Cedars Estates at that time: 19 properties had been completed since the start of the decade, all on the north-east side of Cedars Road and a similar number would be built on the north-west side in the next four years.

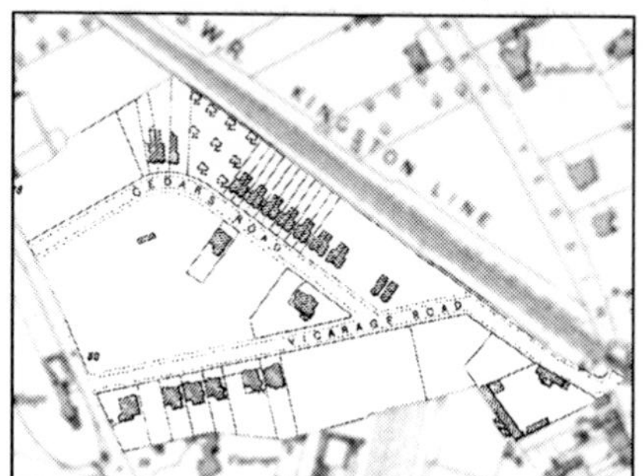

The first two developers to complete properties in the 1890's had so far only used part of their land holding, and they now built on the remainder. John George Pick filled in the gap between *Eavescote* (Number 48) and *Cedar Villas* by erecting two pairs of six-room semi-detached houses (Numbers 40-46, picture on page 131). Unlike the floor plan of earlier semi-detached houses with their wide frontage but narrower back extensions, Pick's houses maintained full width from front to back making for larger rooms and more generous corridors and landings. This change in layout applies to all subsequent semis built on the Estate and may reflect the dwindling presence of live-in servants in middle class houses. Each property had a two-storey square bay topped with its own gabled roof running from front to back of the building together with a cross gable for the front bedroom and dormers for the secondary bedrooms behind. The upper storey was coated in roughcast and is - at least, currently - painted white. The internal porch has a round arch and a single step.

At Number 54/56 (picture on page 133), James Arnold built another pair of semi-detached houses next to his earlier development. However, unlike the one-bay facade of the previous design, these followed a more conventional two-bay design with front entrances in a halls-together configuration protected by an internal porch. The distinctive geometric framework using red and yellow bricks already noted on the neighbouring property is seen again not only here but also on the next four properties Numbers 58-64 (picture on page 133). All are seven-room detached houses occupying a half-plot and sharing a common design, with the exception that Number 58 has its front door on the right whilst, for the other three, it is on the left. There is little of particular interest beyond the usual single-storey canted bay with hipped roof and round arched internal porch, save for the single gable window to light the attic. Numbers 60 - 64 were owned by Belchambers, Number 60 by George Belchamber for his own occupation and Numbers 62-64 by his older brother Robert John as an investment property. (Robert John Belchamber was, for many years, proprietor of the village Post Office and also a long-serving Chairman of the local Urban District Council.)

Continuing to the north western end of Cedars Road: Numbers 66/68 (picture on page 135) is another pair of semi-detached seven-room houses. It is typical of the late-Victorian period complete with its arts and crafts touches of roughcast on the upper storey and hung clay tiles on the gable end above the upstairs windows. The developer was the then vicar Rev W W Wheeler Archer. Number 70 (*Newlyn*) is a detached six-room property commissioned by Robert John Sivers (see page 81) with a range of styles: the ornate capitals on the pilasters of the stone window surrounds on the two-storey bay hark back to earlier neoclassical fashions whilst the roughcast on the gable end is more à la mode. At first glance Number 72 (*Welwyn*) seems to be the same design as its neighbour but with different details and finishes - however the difference in the roof pitches suggest the differences are more than superficial.

The final plot at this end of the road is occupied by Numbers 74/76 another pair of semi-detached six-room houses with an interesting use of a gable centred over the two upper storey windows rather than over the bay.

Returning to the south-east side of Cedars Road, the gap in the 1895 map between Numbers 4 and 12 was filled in with another pair of semi-detached houses (Numbers 8/10) identical to Numbers 12/14 and 16/18 (pictures on page 127) whilst the remaining plot became the site of a three-storey eight-room detached house (*Esk House* Number 6) with a red brick facade and (cheaper) yellow bricks for the rest of the structure. Finally, next door to his Numbers 2 and 4 Cedars Road but actually designated Number 6 Vicarage Road, Hezekiah Newman built his own house, *Ellesmere* (picture on page 201), which was a three-bay version of his other two houses, having central internal porch flanked by two single-storey canted bays. Also on Vicarage Road, another 11-room Brereton mansion was built at Number 35 and called *Manor House*. The owner was Mary Wilkins who had previously lived in the

13-room *Park Gate* at Number 47 so could be said to be down-sizing. *Manor House* was demolished in the 1970s to make way for the entrance to Vineyard Row. Another addition to the housing stock in the middle of the decade was at Numbers 11/13 (*Stoneywood* and *Fintray* picture on page 200) where a pair of seven-room semi-detached houses were built by Peter Wilson. Until 1966, all owners of *Fintray* have insisted on its number being 11a rather than 13

At the end of the decade, those remaining parts of The Cedars Estate that were still owned by Thomas Henry Burroughes were put up for auction. The catalogue for the sale, which took place on 18 July 1899, listed five freehold houses, the ground rents for a further four leasehold houses and 27 plots of freehold building land. The plan issued with the catalogue (see figure 8 on page 98) shows that 18 of the plots are in the centre of the land skirted by Cedars, Vicarage and Park Roads with a further nine on the southern side of Vicarage Road. The plan also conveniently confirms all the properties that had been built by the time of the sale.

Other developments

Although most of the building activity was taking place on The Cedars Estate, new properties were appearing elsewhere on the west side of Hampton Wick. Around 1892, William Henry Wheeler developed Number 9/11 St John's Road with a pair of semi-detached houses known respectively as *Sarnia* and *Rathmore House*. Building right next door to the very large, and elaborate *de la Pierre Villas* built 30 years before (see page 76) did not

Sarnia/Rathmore House

intimidate Wheeler or his architect, and they conceived a similarly large structure with the two houses ranged over four floors including a semi-basement and attics and each having eight-rooms. They mirrored the three-storey bay windows of the neighbour but the high gables of the former gave way to simple dormers not centred over the bays (though these may well have been added subsequently). Rather than compete with the fancy brick, stone and ornamentation, Wheeler went for a stucco finish with decorative mouldings below the sills. Wheeler's first tenant in Number 9 was Frederick Farrow Frecker, a clerk at the Ottoman Bank who, having been born in Guernsey, named the house *Sarnia* - the Latin name for his birthplace.

Meanwhile, Alfred Huntingford - son of Jesse (see page 68) - who lived in *Garden Cottages* off Park Road, decided to dispense with the broad lane previously leading up to his cottages and make do instead with a narrow path (which today allows access to the end of Vineyard Row, partly built on the site of the *Garden Cottages*). In the space released he built a pair of four-room semi-detached houses - Numbers 78/80 Park Road - which he completed in 1896 and which he named *Park Hatch*, placing the name and date prominently between the middle two windows in the upper storey. The four-bay structure is taller than its neighbours either side. Built of yellow and red brick and with pebbledash on the upper storey, the most noticeable external feature is the skillion roof running the width of the building supported on five wooden columns with brackets which provides a covered external porch and shade for the west-facing windows.

Park Hatch

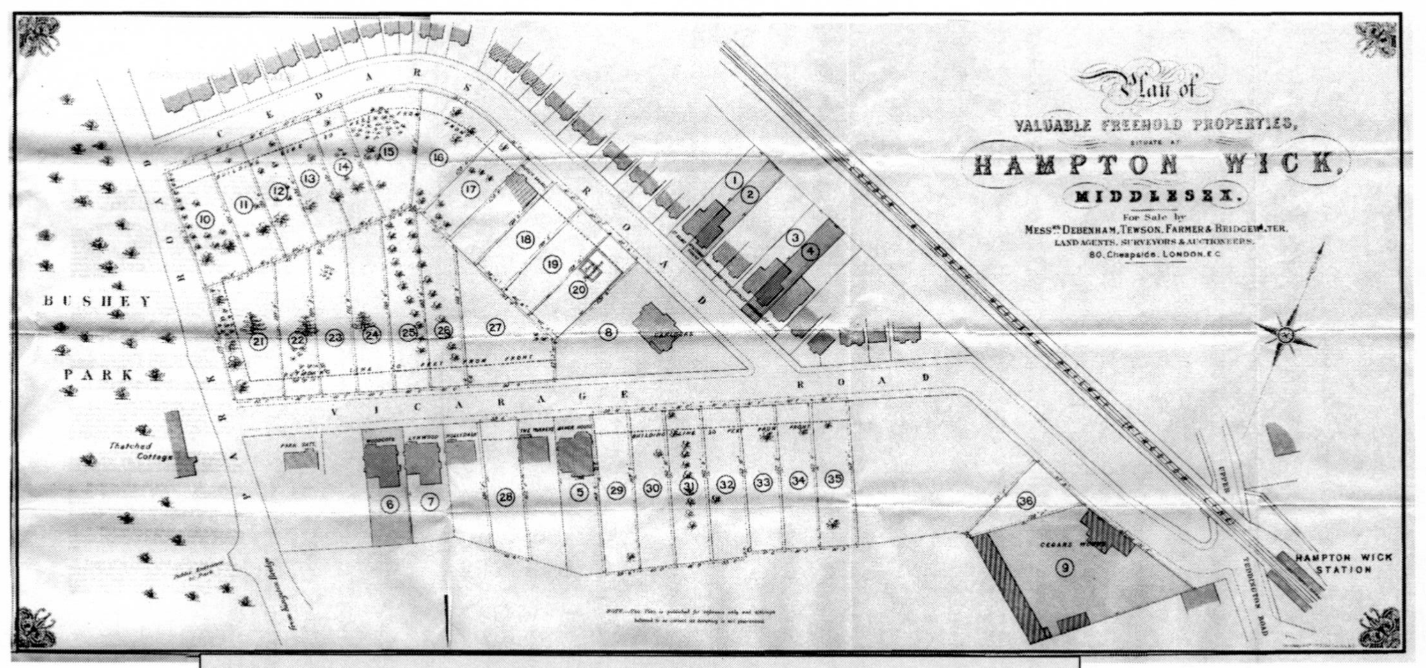

Figure 8: This beautifully drawn map was produced to accompany the Sale Catalogue for the auction of five properties, four freehold ground rents and 27 building plots held on 18th July 1899 when Thomas Burroughes remaining interests in the Cedars Estate were being liquidated.

The 1900s

Cedars Estate

Following the 1899 auction, the first plot to be developed was numbered 10 (see plan opposite) on the south-west corner of Cedars Road and Sandy Lane. The developer was George John Chapple a 55-year-old builder who had previously lived on Vauxhall Bridge Road for over 20 years. His creation at Number 35 Cedars Road, which he called *Bulinga* (presumably after Bulinga Street which was close to his previous house) was designed to impress with its size and ornateness. Externally, the red brick three-storey building had extensive magpie work set in white roughcast in the gable ends on all four facades whilst internally it had eleven rooms. The house was demolished and replaced in 2011.

Bulinga

Plot 17, next to *Rudder Grange*, was next to be developed becoming *Winton* and *Mayfield* at Numbers 5/7. Almost in complete contrast to *Bulinga*, this pair of semi-detached houses (picture on page 130) appear unassuming and conservative in design but, deceptively, they each have seven-rooms, such that Annie How ran *Mayfield* as a boarding house in its early years. Curiously, Plot 16 remained undeveloped until the 1980's. Plot 15 became a pair of seven-room semi-detached houses known as *Killcorel* and *Swanmore*, Numbers 15/17 . They were a conventional Edwardian design with two-storey square bays topped with a gable containing magpie work. One unusual feature was the inclusion of an oriel window in the side wall of each house. The developer was Moses Howell who shortly before had created another pair of houses on Plot 11 known as Numbers 31/33 *Culroy* and *Glennelly*. The designs are so similar without being identical that it suggests they came from the same architect. Plot 14 was the site of Numbers 19/21 *Thurlaston* and *Lutterworth* (picture on page 132). Although built as late as 1907, they retain characteristic late Victorian features including two-storey canted bay with hipped roof. Plot 13 was developed in 1905 as a pair of substantial eight-roomed semi-detached houses with two-storey square bays capped with prominent gabled roofs . There is a single large protruding double porch covering the two adjacent front doors which also has a gabled roof supported by an elaborate wooden structure consisting of mouldings, turnings and fretwork. These properties are Numbers 23/25 Cedars Road and were originally known as *Inverin* and *Brampfort.*

Plots 22 and 23 were developed in 1904 to accommodate two pairs of very substantial semi-detached houses - Numbers 32/34 and 28/30 respectively (left) - curiously, although apparently identical, they were described by three of the occupiers in the 1911 Census as variously having seven, eight or nine rooms! A total of 2,700 sq ft (250 sq metres) of floor space is provided over two floors and an attic. Externally, each house is two bays wide and is arranged in a halls-together configuration. Red brick is used on the lower storey and roughcast above with a prominent string course of saw-tooth brickwork separating the two. The two-storey four-light canted bay is surmounted by a gable with vertical magpie work and a gable window. The super-wide, inset porches have stone pilasters and capitals and the segmental arch also has a keystone. Above the porch is a window and above that is a large dormer surmounted by a smaller replica of the adjacent gable above the main bay. The two buildings are not, in fact, exactly identical, the main difference being that Numbers

32-38 Vicarage Road

32/34 have oriel windows above the porch, unlike their neighbours - but these may not be original.

5-9 Vicarage Road

An interesting development took place at the south-eastern end of Vicarage Road around 1907. At first glance, Numbers 5 - 9 Vicarage Road appear to be a terrace of three identical houses. In fact, it appears from directory and Census information that Number 5 was built in 1898 and lived in by George Smithson, Company Clerk at the Omnibus Works next door. It was known as *The Cottage*, and the 1901 Census describes it as such and mentions it being part of the Omnibus Works. Numbers 7/9 were then built in 1907 as a pair of five-room semi-detached houses, but abutting on Number 5 to form a terrace.

The Parish Land is redeveloped

During the late 1870s John Spink and his sons made three land purchases in the north west of Hampton Wick, beyond *The Cedars*, consisting of a house and a cottage, both with gardens as well as the two triangular areas of land known as the Pepper Pieces which until then had been the property of the Parish. They subsequently sold the house and cottage to the Hampton Court United Gas Works. During the 1880s, the Spinks built four substantial houses at the western-most end of their land holding, filling the smaller triangle and spilling into the start of the larger triangle. The size of these properties can only be deduced from their rateable value as no photographs have so far been found to record what they looked like before they were demolished to make way for *Harrowdene Gardens* in the 1970s and *Fallow Court* the following decade. In the late 1890s John's son, Henry Spink, started work on a development of 12 houses which comprises Numbers 6 to 28 Sandy Lane. All houses were identical in design, but most have been altered and extended over the years. All except the properties at each end have long plots down to the railway line and, with the original building being placed towards the front, equidistant from the side boundaries and fitting into only about half the width, the scope for change is greater than usual as shown by *Deer Lodge*, a Care Home with 12 single rooms built within the original plot at Number 22. Amongst the most original is Number 20 *Lyndhurst*. Using this as a model for the original row of houses, shows that each was a seven-room gable-roof house on two floors with a cross-gable section at the rear extending slightly from both sidewalls. The two-bay configuration places the front entrances to the left and two-storey canted bay windows to the right. The facades are made of red brick with yellow brick used for the rest of the structure. The stone window surrounds on the bay feature pronounced pilasters and capitals whilst the sills are supported on brackets. The front gable end, covered in roughcast, has a small clerestory set in the centre.

Lyndhurst, 20 Sandy Lane

St John's Road

Soon after Henry Spink completed his row of traditional middle class houses on Sandy Lane, another row of properties was under construction on St John's Road. However the origin and purpose of this second row could not have been more different from the first. When the London United Tramways (LUT) lodged their

Tramway Flats

Parliamentary Bill in November 1899 to establish a network of routes between Twickenham and Hampton Court, they faced a significant task of negotiating with the series of local authorities whose jurisdiction lay along the route. In general, the arrival of the trams was welcomed as a catalyst for renovation of an area and a source of capital to fund such work. This was particularly the case in Hampton Wick where the necessity to widen the High Street to accommodate two lines of track would lead to the elimination and replacement of a large amount of dilapidated property. However, the Hampton Wick Urban District Council surely excelled themselves when they persuaded LUT to build the row of ten *Tramway Flats* at Numbers 14-32 St John's Road in part compensation for the dozens of properties that had been demolished. The people rehoused were those residents of the ten properties on the east side of the High Street opposite The Foresters that were removed in early 1903. Eight out of the ten agreed to the move into St John's Road. They became tenants of LUT, an arrangement that lasted until at least 1915. The layout chosen for the new properties was most unusual and almost unique. Externally the building appears to be a conventional terrace of five units with a halls-together configuration. The front is red

top: These early-Georgian tenements (arrowed) were demolished (above) to make room for the tramway. Eight of the ten displaced families accepted new homes in the *Tramway Flats* on St John's Road.

brick on the lower storey and roughcast on the upper storey, separated by a string course of dentilated brickwork. The windows are four-paned sashes, the ground floor being unusual in being arranged in a very shallow cant bay with hipped roof but set under a segmental arch constructed with two courses of header bricks laid on their side (i.e. rowlocks). A similar construction is used for the inset porches which have round arches. The unique aspect of the design is revealed within the porches where two front doors are placed side-by-side within a common inset porch. One of these opens onto a narrow straight staircase leading to the upper property. Since each unit has its own street door, this configuration is officially described as a "half-house". The internal design has a four-room arrangement of 750 sq ft (70 sq metres) by virtue of including a deep rear extension. In his Summary Book, the 1911 Census Enumerator describes the block as "Workmen's Model Dwellings", perhaps showing the esteem in which the development was held within Hampton Wick.

The land on which the *Tramway Flats* were built was formerly part of the front garden of *Maude Cottage* Number 10 St John's Road. William Henry Wheeler acquired this property from its previous owner John William Reed in 1895 and renamed it *Clennon.* Wheeler and his father already owned several properties on both sides of St John's Road, so this was a natural fit within their portfolio, especially as they owned *Grove Cottages* at the other end of the garden. Wheeler himself lived in the house himself for a couple of years. However, he was a developer, not a sentimentalist and, once he had decided to move out (whilst still retaining ownership), he lost no time in disposing of the garden. The first transaction involved the plot nearest the house. This was bought by Albert Bullen who built *St John's Foundry* at the end of the plot, opened in 1897. Bullen had been a gas plumber with a shop at 2 High Street. The foundry, which was used for making brass castings, was the next stage of his business plan and its success can be measured by the fact that he closed the shop in 1905 to concentrate on the foundry, moving into the house he had just built on the rest of the plot. Called *Saxby*, at Number 12 St John's Road, it is a six-room red brick structure with a square ground floor bay on the left side and an inset porch with elaborate stone pediment within its gothic arch. The mullions are shaped as slender stone columns.

Wheeler's second transaction involved the larger plot to the southwest, most of which, as has been seen, was acquired by LUT for the *Tramway Flats*. However, Bullen retained the strip furthest from the road to give himself room for future expansion.

Sandy Lane

The *Thatched House* (see page 35) was built with two matching coach houses/stables at the north end of its grounds. By 1910, these had been converted into four small residences known as *Sandy Lane Cottages* Numbers 5 - 9 (below). A recent resident said he had been told that the conversions were done at her own expense by Ann Hudson, sometime landlady of *The Foresters* as an investment to fund her retirement but was later dismayed to find that The Crown, as landlords, simply reclaimed the converted properties without any compensation.

Sandy Lane Cottages

The 1910s

With confidence in the economic outlook on the wane and growing uncertainty over European stability, house building almost ceased during the 1910s. The only property to be developed was Numbers 26/28 Church Grove, a pair of five-room semi-detached houses with single-storey square bay windows at the front covered by a single hipped roof and with side entrances. The developer was Christopher Charles Wren who for the previous ten years had been the tenant of the Grove Inn at 60 High Street. Wren and his wife decided for a change in direction and bought the land in the angle between Church Grove and Park Road. This had hitherto been owned by the occupiers of Number 40 and Number 38 Park Road and been used as additional gardens. Wren built the current pair of houses on Number 38's garden but had to wait until 1920 before he could develop on Number 40's garden. He had the distinction of being the last developer to build before,and the first developer to build after the First World War. However, he showed his determination for a new future by describing his occupation in the 1911 Census as being simply "House Owner".

26/28 Church Grove

The 1920s

Church Grove

As soon as hostilities ended, Christopher Wren lost no time in restarting his development plan. On the larger garden plot that had previously belonged to the owners of 40 Park Road he built a terrace of three two-storey houses. In reality, it was a pair of semi-detached houses (Numbers 32/34 Church Grove) and a single double-fronted house (Number 30 Church Grove) attached on the south-east side into which Wren himself moved as soon as it was completed. He named the properties *Flemish Villas*, but the connection with Flanders was not geographic but lapine: Wren was a very enthusiastic rabbit breeder and specialised in the Flemish Giant variety, so named because of its origin and the fact that it can grow to 80cm long and weigh up to 10 kg.

Flemish Villas under construction

Two new developments further along Church Grove resulted from the sale of land from the garden of *The Limes* at Number 10. Since 1900, this property had been owned by Charles Henry Notley. In 1924, the building was undergoing conversion into flats, and Notley chose to sell off the surplus land in two lots. Roland Burton bought the plot immediately next door and built *The Firs*. He moved in in 1926. Two years later, Notley concluded a deal for £470 to sell a strip 40 ft x 165 ft to the Diocese of London which was to become the site for the *St John the Baptist Church* Hall. The foundation stone was laid on 25 June 1927 by the Princess Royal. Having completed the ceremony and entering into the paddock opposite (which had been prepared for the Church Fete), she declared it open. Later the same afternoon she presented the paddock to Hampton Wick parish as a gift from her father, King George V. Now known as the Kings Field, it was later laid out as a playground for the young with tennis courts and football pitches.

Recently it has become a skate-boarding Mecca. The church hall was completed on 15 October 1927 at a cost of £6,000. It was named Ronayne Hall as a tribute to the very popular incumbent Rev Ronald Ronayne (seen below with the Princess Royal).

Vicarage Road

During the 1920s, all the undeveloped land on the southern side of Vicarage Road between Number 11a and Number 35 was covered with a total of 11 properties. Apart from two pairs of semi-detached -

Numbers 13a/15 and 17/19 - all the houses were detached. Numbers 23, 25 and 33 were clearly created by the same (unknown) developer and are in a distinctive chalet style of architecture emphasised by shutters on the lower windows on some and heavy exposed timbers on the upper half. (They are technically semi-bungalows.) Numbers 27 - 31 also share their design which features an asymmetric gable and round arch motif above the main upstairs window mirroring the arch above the front door.

Park Road

Almost exactly one hundred years after the sale of Lot 6 at auction (see page 22), development of this remaining piece of the original Wick Green now began. A set of five houses arranged as a pair of semi-detached and a terrace of three were built on either side of what is now the vehicle entrance to Park Court. At first glance, the design seems the same across all five, but in fact the semis have slate hipped roofs above their two-storey square bays, whereas *The Terrace* has tiled gables. All five were first occupied in 1925 and were known as Numbers 42-50 Park Road. Their arrival caused all houses beyond them to be renumbered. The names chosen by their owners were *Sans Souci, Wyke, Waipiro, Sunny View* and *Angley.* Life in those first few years would not have been very peaceful as huge quantities of ballast were being extracted and transported away by lorry from the ground behind.

Hampton Wick Developers 7. The Offer Family

Harry Offer (b.1876) was the second son of James Offer who had founded a business as a builder in Kingston in 1873 and pioneered the installation of gas and electric lighting in Kingston houses. His elder brother James managed the on-site work and Harry managed the Works and Office. When the 1914 war caused a slump in building, the resourceful Harry founded the Harry Offer Aircraft Company to build sub-assemblies for Sopwith, the Kingston-based builders of the Sopwith Camel, the most successful fighter of the conflict. After the war Harry returned to the building trade, but now in his own right. However, with the rush of resumed building in the early 1920s, he found the competition cut-throat and withdrew from building construction and specialised in the conversion of (given the shortage of available servants) now excessively-large Edwardian Family Dwellings into much needed flats. When the supply of such properties dried up, he retained the converted flats for letting. This absorbed his available capital but provided a steady income. As capital was rebuilt, shop and commercial property was added to the portfolio for letting.

Harry brought his three sons into the business and ensured they were trained appropriately, Tom as a builder and quantity surveyor (he left when the firm exited building), Jack as a Chartered Surveyor and Dick as an Insurance Broker. Jack and Dick were also accomplished oarsmen and together won both The Goblets event at Henley in 1936 and silver medals in double skulls in the 1938 Empire Games in Australia. When the demand for new residential properties was re-established in the mid-1950s, it became obvious that the family's Edwardian conversions were no longer viable and that the portfolio should be modified. The company demolished and rebuilt most of the old properties to designs by their in-house architect Malcolm Watton.

In 1961 Harry's grandson Tony, on qualifying as a Chartered Surveyor, joined the family business where his enthusiasm for challenges led him and the business into new fields of development in house building in the Kingston area, Malta and Jersey and later into office, shopping and industrial development. In 1974 the house building side of the business was sold to the Higgs and Hill Group based in New Malden. Malcolm Watten transferred with that operation and became a Director. Tony's son Tim - great-grandson of the founder - now heads the family firm as it heads towards its centenary as a long-term and highly influential participant in Hampton Wick's development.

The 1930s

Although only five buildings were constructed in this decade (compared with 20 in the previous) more than one 100 new households were nonetheless accommodated. The answer to this apparent conundrum was the arrival in Hampton Wick of a new type of accommodation: the purpose-built block of flats. The Central Government's drive to create Lloyd George's promised "Homes for Heroes" led to a surge in demand for new housing. However, the shortage of remaining virgin building land - evident in Hampton Wick as much as elsewhere in the country - led to the adoption of flats as the dominant form of accommodation. Expediency may have been the catalyst, but the perceived acceptability - indeed desirability - of this housing solution meant that Hampton Wick acquired and filled more than 100 flats some two decades before its neighbours in Teddington and Hampton adopted similar schemes. Two development schemes were responsible for this change - *Park Court* and *Ingram House* - and construction on both started in 1936.

Park Court

Three four-storey blocks - containing 32, 24 and 16 flats respectively - faced inwards and were built around the perimeter of the site to provide firm foundations since the centre itself had been recently used as a quarry. Each set of staircases provides access to eight flats. The clean rectangular lines of the design are emphasised by the wide windows, continuous brick lintels and stepped parapets. The only visible curve is in the simple angled canopy above each entrance door. (Interestingly, this exact design had previously appeared in an application for a development on Glamorgan Road which never materialised.) The developers built and opened each block in succession over the course of two years. The 1938 Kelly's Directory lists a full set of 72 residents' names indicating how complete was the take-up of this new housing option.

Ingram House

The development consists of a main four-storey block containing 24 flats and smaller replica at right angles with a further eight flats. The style is much more of an elaborate art deco mansion block than the utilitarian structure of Park Court and the inclusion of balconies, projecting bays and the full-height round arches fronting each stairwell creates a very attractive design. This up-market development occupied the site of the former Vicarage with its views across to Bushy Park. Presumably this was reflected in its prices and the speed of occupation was markedly slower than with Park Court: only one resident listed in the 1937 Directory, seven in 1938, 19 in 1939 and 31 out of a possible 32 by 1940.

Cedars Estate

Little else was constructed in the decade apart from a bungalow (since demolished) on Plot 28 and a pair of semi-detached houses on Plot 24 now known as Numbers 20/22 Vicarage Road - which introduced the first rounded bay windows to Hampton Wick.

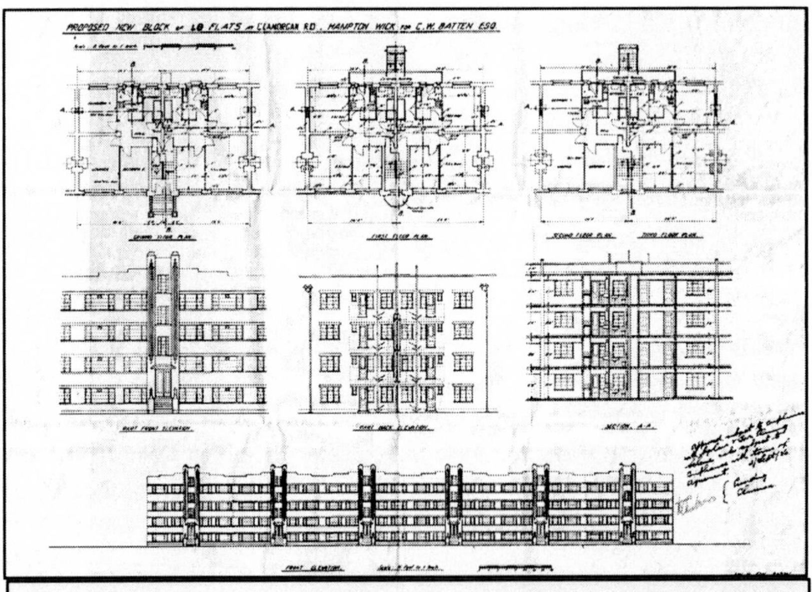

above: The original planning application, approved by the local authority, was to build the block of 48 flats on Glamorgan Road not Park Road.

The 1940s

Unsurprisingly nothing was built during the years of the Second World War - but nothing was apparently destroyed either. This is unexpected given that there were already a number of troops and support staff accommodated in the north-east section of Bushy Park which - if the records are to be believed - is the one area that received no bombs (see below). One bomb is recorded as having fallen in the area of the church, but all pre-war buildings appear to have been intact so it may not have actually exploded.

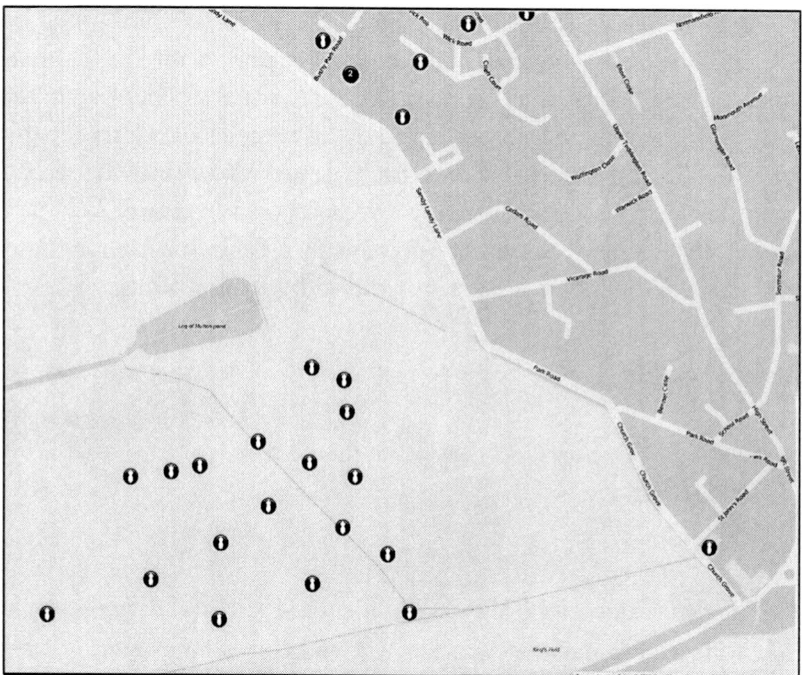

above: A map of the bombs that fell on the west side of Hampton Wick during The Blitz 7th October 1940 - 6th June 1941

Source: The Bomb Site Project

The 1950s

Only one development took place in this decade, but it was an intriguing one involving Plots 18, 19, and 20 on Cedars Road and Plot 27 on Vicarage Road (see Figure 8 page 96). A pair of bungalows was immediately built on Plots 19 and 20 and a detached house (Number 18 Vicarage Road) built in 1954 on Plot 27. Furthermore, a broad strip of land at the western side of Plot 27, in a line from the corner of the existing garden of *Rudder Grange* to Vicarage Road, was carved out and added to that garden (an arrangement that still exists today). The final piece of the jigsaw is that another bungalow was later (1967) built on Plot 18. It is possible that all of these plots (together with Plot 26) may once have all belonged to the owner of *Rudder Grange* since one of the bungalows was immediately occupied by his namesake - presumably his son. The developer was almost certainly named Viney since the second bungalow,and the detached house were occupied by Harry W Viney and Harry S Viney respectively (presumably a father/son combination) and the 1967-built bungalow was occupied by Lynton Viney.

The 1960s

The demolition of the Vicarage in the mid-1930s and its replacement with a new building was the first and, for a long time, isolated example of the recycling of a building plot. Developers argued that old houses did not contain the sort of accommodation demanded by modern householders (see The Offer Family article on page 110) and, even when divided into flats, did not make such efficient use of the plot that a new purpose-built replacement could offer. They were supported in this opinion by the local authority planners who needed to cater for an expanding population in their area - or risk losing it and the income it generated. Thus many of the larger properties whose creation has been described in earlier pages of this book became targets for redevelopment. This process effectively began in the 1960s and has only recently been checked by increasing awareness of the need to conserve and recycle existing buildings on both commercial and environmental grounds.

Church Grove was a natural starting point since it contained several large mansions in prestigious positions. Demolition of the buildings on the corner of Church Grove and Hampton Court Road in 1960 made space for the construction of the seven-storey Kingston Bridge House, the first purpose-built office building - and the first use of concrete as a building material - in Hampton Wick. Later, in 1965, two of the largest properties at Numbers 10 and 12 Church Grove were demolished to make way for *Heron House*, a five-storey development by local developer Riverside Development Ltd (part of The Offer Group see page 110) comprising 21 flats.

On the Cedars Estate, three of the remaining plots that had been auctioned off in 1899 (see page {Ref}) were finally developed. Respectively, these were plots 24, 18 and 12 on which were built a pair of semi-detached houses at Number 24/26 Vicarage Road (1960), a building containing three flats at Number 27/29 and a bungalow called *Griffon* next to *Rudder Grange* (1967). Meanwhile a development of four flats - Numbers 36 to 42 Vicarage Road - was completed in the garden on the west side of the extra-wide plot 21.

The last, and by far the largest, of the 1960s projects was the creation of *Harrowdene Gardens* by Wates Built Homes Ltd. The development consisted of 132 properties on a former wetland site - mainly in Teddington - that was drained during the Second World War to accommodate railways

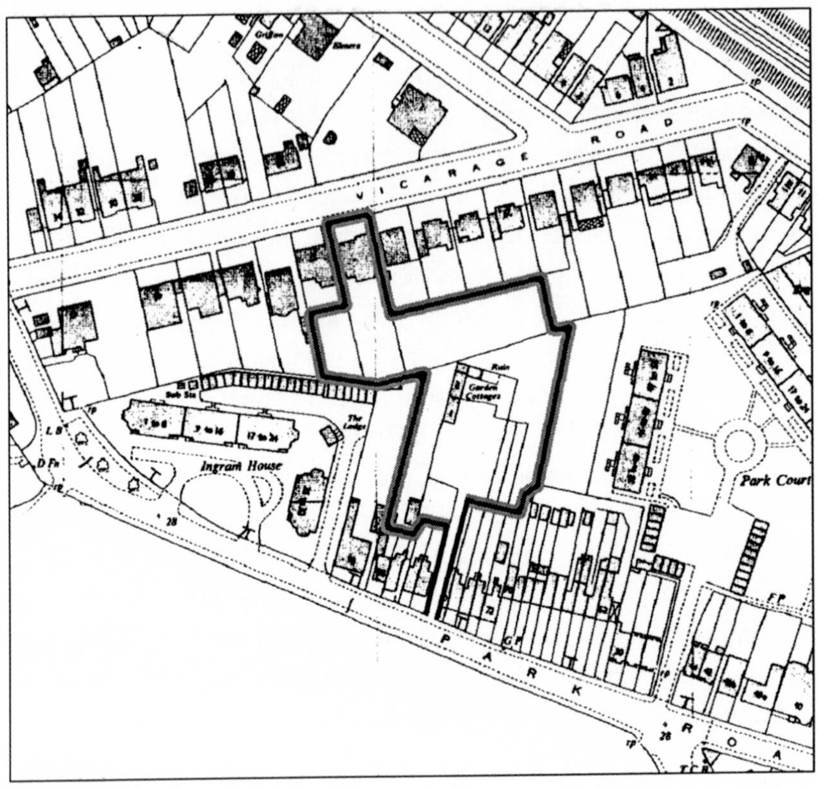

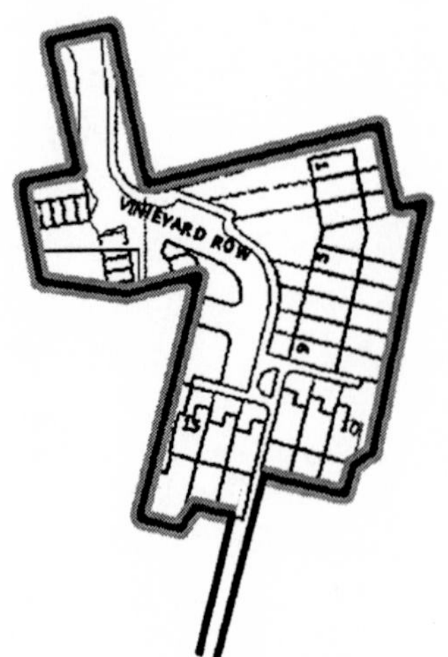

above:
In making space for Vineyard Row, only two properties were demolished to create the site for 15 houses.
left: Careful planning ensured full use was made of the available space.

sidings for the military camps in Bushy Park. Though most of the site was derelict, the section lying within Hampton Wick contained three large houses - *Everdon, Dalton* and *Warren Lodges* - built in the late 1880s by John Spinks. The scheme was completed in 1969.

The 1970s

Two developments took place during this decade, each involving the demolition of previous large mansions and the redevelopment of their plots. Both were undertaken by Offers and their architect Malcolm Watton (see page 110).

The first was the creation in 1974 of Vineyard Row as a cul de sac off the south side of Vicarage Road. The site was created by the demolition of Number 35 Vicarage Road (*Manor House*) together with *Garden Cottages*, four old tenements that were mentioned by Ayliffe in his youthful memoirs (page 29). These were accessed from between Numbers 80 and 82 Park Road. These plots - and several other small pieces of previously undeveloped land - were skilfully merged to provide the site for 15 three-bedroom terraced town houses each with their own lock-up garage (see opposite).

The second development was completed a year later when the 15-room mansion on the south-west corner of Vicarage Road and Cedars Road, known as *Carlogas*, was demolished to make way for *Eisenhower House*, a 16-flat development (see pictures on page 203). The building was named to commemorate General Dwight D Eisenhower, the Supreme Commander of the Allied Expeditionary Force, whose headquarters in early 1944 were in nearby Bushy Park

The 1980s

In 1983, plot 16 from the 1899 Cedars Estate sale was finally built upon as Numbers 13/15 Cedars Road, a pair of semi-detached houses, were constructed. It seems odd that this corner site should have remained available for so long.

Cedars House (not to be confused with *The Cedars*) at Number 2 Sandy Lane had been built around 1880 by John Spink. The Hampton Court United Gas Company bought the property in 1895 and it was home to William Comly Lamb, the Company Secretary, for over 30 years. The property was retained through the 1948 gas industry nationalisation but after SEEBOARD, its last industrial owner, was refused permission to turn its grounds into a staff car park, they sold the property. The house was demolished in 1985 and five townhouses erected in its place.

In 1989, the last of the four largest houses built by John Spink around 1890 was demolished (the other three had disappeared in 1969 as part of the *Harrowdene Gardens* project). A development of five three-storey terraced townhouses (designed by Malcolm Watton) were constructed and given street addresses of Numbers 30 - 38 Sandy Lane.

The 1990s

In 1993 the Twickenham-based property developer St George PLC applied for permission to build seven new houses on land at the rear of Number 34 St John's Road. The application and the subsequent appeal were rejected on the basis that the proposal included plans to demolish everything already on the site. The land in question certainly had an interesting history having originally housed the stable block for *The Limes*, the 1860s-built 15-room mansion at Number 10 Church Grove. The stable was accessed from St John's Road. When the owner sold the block at the end of the First World War, it began a very varied career, First used as a printing works, it later became a motor engineering works. From 1935 to 1958 it was the Wick Boarding Kennels before reverting to motor engineering, notably for a period as FWD (i.e. four wheel drive) specialising in renovating Series 2 Land Rovers. The objection to the St George proposal was that it included the demolition of the original stable block so their 1995 application, which now included just five new houses together with conversion of the original building, was accepted and the first residents moved in to *Saddlers Mews* the following year.

Another development involving a stable building took place in 1997. *Fairlight Mews* at Number 15 St John's Road was originally, as its name implies, the coach and stable block for *Fairlight* at Number 4 Church Grove. Ownership had remained with the main property and the proprietor used it to build replica Jaguar D-types. In 1997 planning permission was granted to convert the premises into a three-bedroom live/work unit and it has since been home to a sound recording studio business

2000 to the present day

St John's Road

Two developments have been completed since 2000, coincidentally both contiguous with *Fairlight Mews* (see above) and both involving live/work units. The site at Number 13 St John's Road has long been used for commercial and industrial purposes, already being shown on the 1863 Ordnance Survey map when it was used as a coal and corn storage yard by John Plow Smith. From 1921 it was occupied by the premises of Eland Engineering for the design and manufacturing of hydraulic oil equipment. In 1998 the company decided it needed to move into larger premises but required the proceeds from the sale of its Hampton Wick site as residential development to fund such a move. Planning permission was refused (the company was later dissolved) on the grounds that the site must continue to offer employment opportunities. The compromise (won on appeal) was the construction of seven live/work units, now known as *St John's Mews.* Meanwhile, next door, at 11a St John's Road, a new three-storey live/work unit replaced a single-storey unit in an unusual design (see picture on page 192) that maximises use of the very compact site.

Cedars Estate

Five new developments have taken place. Richmond Housing Trust built Abigail Court at Number 2 - 4 Vicarage Road, a seven-flat development replacing a large 1890s house that from 1910 - 1940 had been used as a Scattered Home for Children (an early form of care in the community) and later provided more conventional social housing. New developments at Numbers 37a/b and 45a/b Vicarage Road have both seen multi-unit semi-detached properties replacing single 1970s bungalows. Most recently, *Park Gate* Number 47 Vicarage Road on its south-east corner with Sandy Lane has been extensively refurbished as a single family home - albeit with eight bedrooms and three sitting rooms. In the same timeframe, the house in the equivalent position in Cedars Road (see page 99) has been replaced by a new glass and steel construction containing seven two-bedroomed flats constructed by Richmond Churches Housing Trust. Also included in the scheme was a new four-bedroomed house in the garden fronting onto Sandy Lane and named *Liberty House.*

The Gasworks Site

By far the biggest new construction project of recent years has been the redevelopment by Linden Homes of the original Hampton Court United Gas Company five acre site on Sandy Lane (most recently owned by SEEboard). This very large area was a market garden before being acquired for the original gasworks in 1850 (see page 22). Production of gas here ended in the 1960s and the gasometers were later removed. The site was then used by SEEBOARD as a depot with workshops, stores and a vehicle parking area. In 1972 they built a three-storey office block (*Beacon House*) at the south end of the site. By the time the first planning application was lodged in 1994, *Beacon House* had been empty for some time and the other (northern) half of the site was being operated by Jewsons as a builders merchants. Since the planning application for the five acre site involved the "demolition of existing buildings and erection of office unit, crèche, nursing home and 198 flats (11 separate new buildings in all)" it is not surprising that the local authority failed to determine the case in time so let it go straight to appeal. Approval was finally given in July 2006. The scheme has been implemented in two phases but only the first (southern) half actually lies within the Hampton Wick boundary.

above: **The Gasworks Site**
This aerial view taken in the 1930s, with the north side of Cedars Road at the bottom, shows both the scale of the site and its proximity to the neighbouring housing. Gas production ceased in the 1960s.

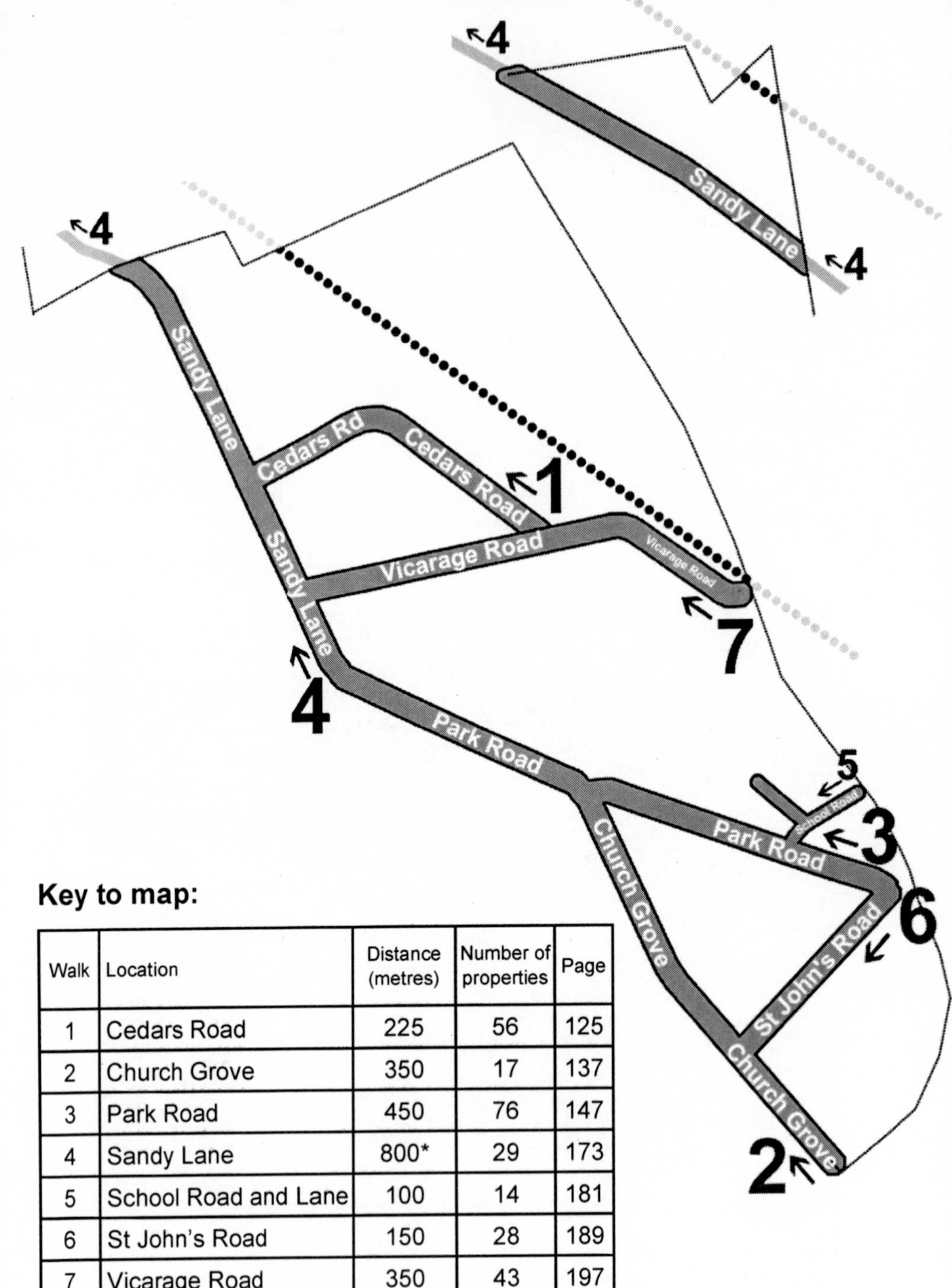

Key to map:

Walk	Location	Distance (metres)	Number of properties	Page
1	Cedars Road	225	56	125
2	Church Grove	350	17	137
3	Park Road	450	76	147
4	Sandy Lane	800*	29	173
5	School Road and Lane	100	14	181
6	St John's Road	150	28	189
7	Vicarage Road	350	43	197

* additional 700 metres to the detached portion (Bushy Park Cottage)

PART TWO: EXPLORING THE PRESENT

Walking Guides

There is so much interest and enjoyment to be had by walking the streets of Hampton Wick with eyes open, curiosity aroused and time to see and enjoy the surroundings. To encourage and inform that interest is the purpose of the remainder of this book.

It is probable that most people think of a street as being primarily a thoroughfare - a place of passage from one location to another. Their principal focus is on getting swiftly and safely to their destination and the immediate surroundings are of little consequence. However, a street is also a public space, bordered by frontages of (mainly) private properties - frequently on both sides of the street. If these properties are of sufficient interest to catch the walker's attention, then the street becomes like a corridor in a museum or gallery - a place where you are more inclined to saunter along, pausing to examine and enjoy one exhibit before moving on to the next. We are fortunate that our streets in Hampton Wick so amply repay time invested in such an approach.

The second half of this book is therefore specifically designed to help those wishing to go out and see what has been bequeathed to us by the former residents, architects, developers, financiers and legislators who helped to create today's Hampton Wick. The material in this section is arranged as a series of seven walks (see opposite), each beginning with a brief overview of the street and its history together with a detailed street plan. The walk starts at house number 1 and describes in words and pictures exactly what is to be seen on each side of the road. For most of the walks, the left hand page refers to the (odd-numbered) building(s) on the walker's left and vice versa. The walker's attention is drawn to English Heritage Listed Buildings and to Buildings of Townscape Merit as designated by the London Borough of Richmond upon Thames. Where appropriate the walker is also referred to relevant material in the first part of the book thus: **[nn]**.

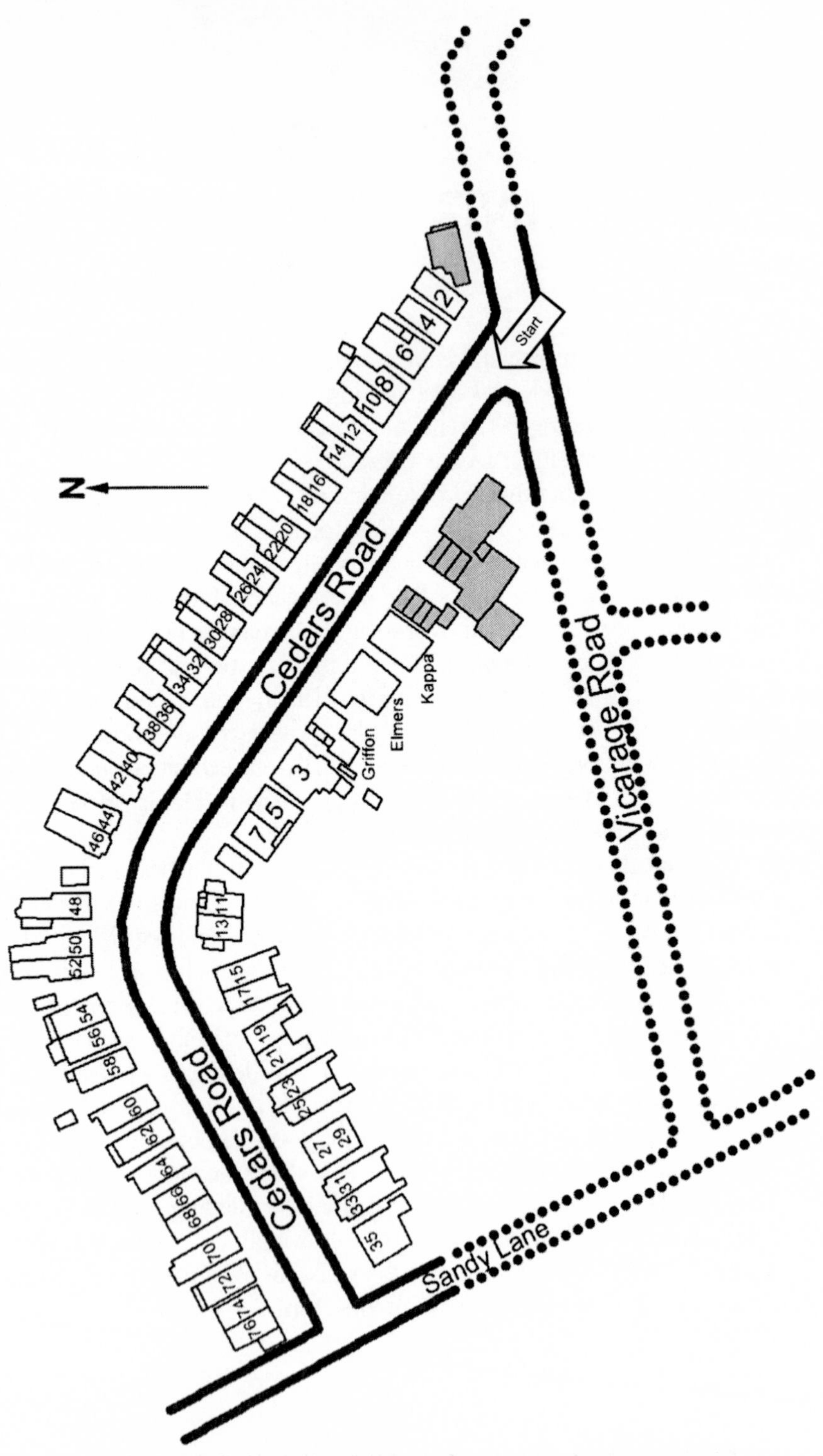
N
Start
Cedars Road
Cedars Road
Vicarage Road
Sandy Lane
Griffon
Elmers
Kappa
2
4
6
8
10
12
14
16
18
20
22
24
26
28
30
32
34
36
38
40
42
44
46
48
50
52
54
56
58
60
62
64
66
68
70
72
74
76
3
5
7
11
13
15
17
19
21
23
25
27
29
31
33
35

CEDARS ROAD

Brick by Brick

Cedars Road, one of the two new thoroughfares created for the Cedars Estate, was opened to the public in October 1893. There were a total of 62 building plots, each 40 feet wide and around 130 feet deep, laid out on the estate. 40 of these were on Cedars Road itself. "Only first-class residences of not less than £700 in value are to be erected upon them" proclaimed the prospectus. However, by 1890, only ten houses had been built on the whole estate and the rules, at least as far as Cedars Road was concerned, were relaxed.

The effect was dramatic. Over the next ten years, 35 residences were built on Cedars Road – 26 semi-detached and nine detached - and every plot on the right (even-numbered) side of the road was occupied. With the exception of the ten *Cedar Villas* (Numbers 20-38), almost all other properties were one-off designs presenting today's explorer in Cedars Road with a splendid gallery of late-Victorian middle class architectural taste.

above: *Eisenhower House,* 8 Vicarage Road
Built in 1975, this 16-flat development was named to honour Gen. Dwight D Eisenhower who, as Supreme Allied Commander in Europe during World War 2, had his headquarters in Bushy Park during the early part of 1944.

below: *Carlogas*, 1 Cedars Road
Built in 1889 and designed by Irish architect Franc Sadleir Brereton, this 15-room mansion was demolished in 1975 to make way for *Eisenhower House*. Note Brereton's signature - the three small round arch blind gable windows - which also feature on his other designs at Number 3 Cedars Road as well as on Numbers 37, 41 and 45 Vicarage Road.

above: *Hesley, Southcote and Devoncot*
2, 4 and 6 Cedars Road

Numbers 2 and 4 were built in 1894 by Hezekiah Newman a dairyman turned property developer who seemed to have the Midas touch. He lived in Number 2 before later building and moving into the neighbouring property in Vicarage Road. Number 6 was built in 1897. Note the original gas lamp standard in its strategic position on the corner.

below: *Abbotsleigh, Shirley, Montrose, Franklyns, 10 Cedar Villas and St Elmo* 8-18 Cedars Road

These three pairs of semi-detached houses were built in 1897. The use of a mansard roof allowed the architect to incorporate two additional full-height attic rooms bringing the total complement up to eight.

above: *Kappa , Elmers and Griffon*
Elmers and *Griffon* were built in 1950 and *Kappa* in 1968 probably on land that had previously belonged to Number 3 *Rudder Grange*.

below: *Rudder Grange,* 3 Cedars Road
Built in 1895 as part of the first ever batch of houses on The Cedars Estate designed by Franc Brereton, *Rudder Grange* was named after a novel by American writer Frank R Stockton (inset) published in 1879 which "recounted the whimsically fantastic and amusing adventures of a family living on a canal boat". Unlike the family in the novel, the residents of *Rudder Grange* enjoyed life in a light and airy house with its many spacious rooms and generous hallways and passages.

above: 6-10 *Cedar Villas* 28-20 Cedars Road

Cedar Villas is the largest single development on Cedars Road, consisting of 10 semi-detached houses of very similar six-room design. Built by John Imray in three phases between 1891-94, the last pair to be built are shown above with the earlier 1892 examples beyond.

below: *Cedar Villas* around 1910

The full set of Imray's ten villas are seen in this postcard view by Young and Co. of Teddington. The earliest examples had magpie work and roughcast infill in their gable ends. This decorative treatment was dispensed with in favour of unadorned brickwork by the time the last examples were built in 1894.

above: *Winton and Mayfield* 5/7 Cedars Road

Built in 1902, these seven-room semi-detached houses were sufficiently spacious for Annie How to run Number 7 as a boarding house for a number of years. Now used as a care home for eight residents.

below: 11-13 Cedars Road

There being no Number 9 in Cedars Road, this 1983-built pair of semi-detached houses are the next properties. They occupy the corner plot, which was had been part of the extensive garden of Numbers 5/7.

above, right to left: *Duncroft/Harpseth and Oakville/Appleby*

40/2 and 44/6 Cedars Road

These two pairs of semi-detached six-room houses were built in 1898 by John George Pick. In the 1901 Census, three of the four properties were lived in by clerks: gas company, solicitor's and Civil Service.

below, right to left: *Evescote and Ivydene/Thornbury*

48 and 50/2 Cedars Road

Evescote was built in 1889 by John George Pick and is unusual in that it only half fills its plot. Pick's first tenant was a stock-jobbing clerk at the London Stock Exchange. *Ivydene/Thornbury* were also built in 1889 by James Arnold, a gas rate collector, who himself then lived in Number 50.

above: *Kilcorrel and Swanmore* 15/17 Cedars Road
These seven-room houses were built in 1902 by Miss Howell who also built Numbers 31/33 using a similar design. Unique to Numbers 15/17 (and to Hampton Wick) are the two-storey bays on the side of each house.

above: *Thurlaston/Lutterworth* 19/21 Cedars Road
Built in Edwardian 1906, these seven-room semi-detached houses nevertheless used a typical late Victorian style. The developer was George James Chamberlin who himself lived in Number 19 with his wife Meta who had been born in Thurlaston.

below: *Inverin/Brampford* 23-25 Cedars Road
Built in 1904, these eight-room semi-detached houses use a halls-together configuration which features a beautiful Edwardian protruding double porch using moulded, turned and fret-worked timber to stunning effect.

above: *Darnlee and Avening* 54/56 Cedars Road

These six-room houses were built by James Arnold in 1896 using a design similar to the one he had employed at Numbers 50/2 (built seven years earlier) but now the entrance doors were placed in the front.

above left to right: *St Aubyns, Rowena, Wentworth and Newstead* 58-64 Cedars Road

These seven-room houses were constructed in 1896/7. Three were built by the Belchamber brothers - Robert John (Numbers 62-64 as an investment) and George (Number 60 for his own occupation). George and Sara Belchamber called their house *Rowena* in memory of their daughter who had just died. Two years later, George himself died at the young age of 36.

left 27/29 Cedars Road

Constructed in 1965 on an empty plot, the building contains two flats and a maisonette.

left *Culroy/Glennelly*

31/33 Cedars Road

Built in 1908 by Miss Howell, these six-room semi-detached houses have many architectural similarities with her other properties at 15/17 Cedars Road.

left: 35 Cedars Road

The present building which contains seven 2-bed flats was completed by Richmond Churches Housing Trust in 2013. It replaces *Bulinga*, an 11-room mansion **[99]** built by its developer George George Chapple in 1899 which can be seen on the extreme right of the c1910 postcard view. *below*

right ***The Cottage/ Polmont Cottage***
66/68 Cedars Road
These seven-room semi-detached houses were built in 1896 by the then Vicar of Hampton Wick, Rev William Wheeler Archer.

right ***Newlyn and Welwyn,***
70 and 72 Cedars Road
These six-room detached houses were built in 1896 by their first residents, Herbert Constable and Robert John Sivers **[81]**.

right ***Cleveland Cottage and Freda Vale,***
74 and 76 Cedars Road
This pair of six-room semi-detached houses were built in 1896 by William Douglas, a warden at Hampton Court Palace. Douglas himself lived in Number 76.

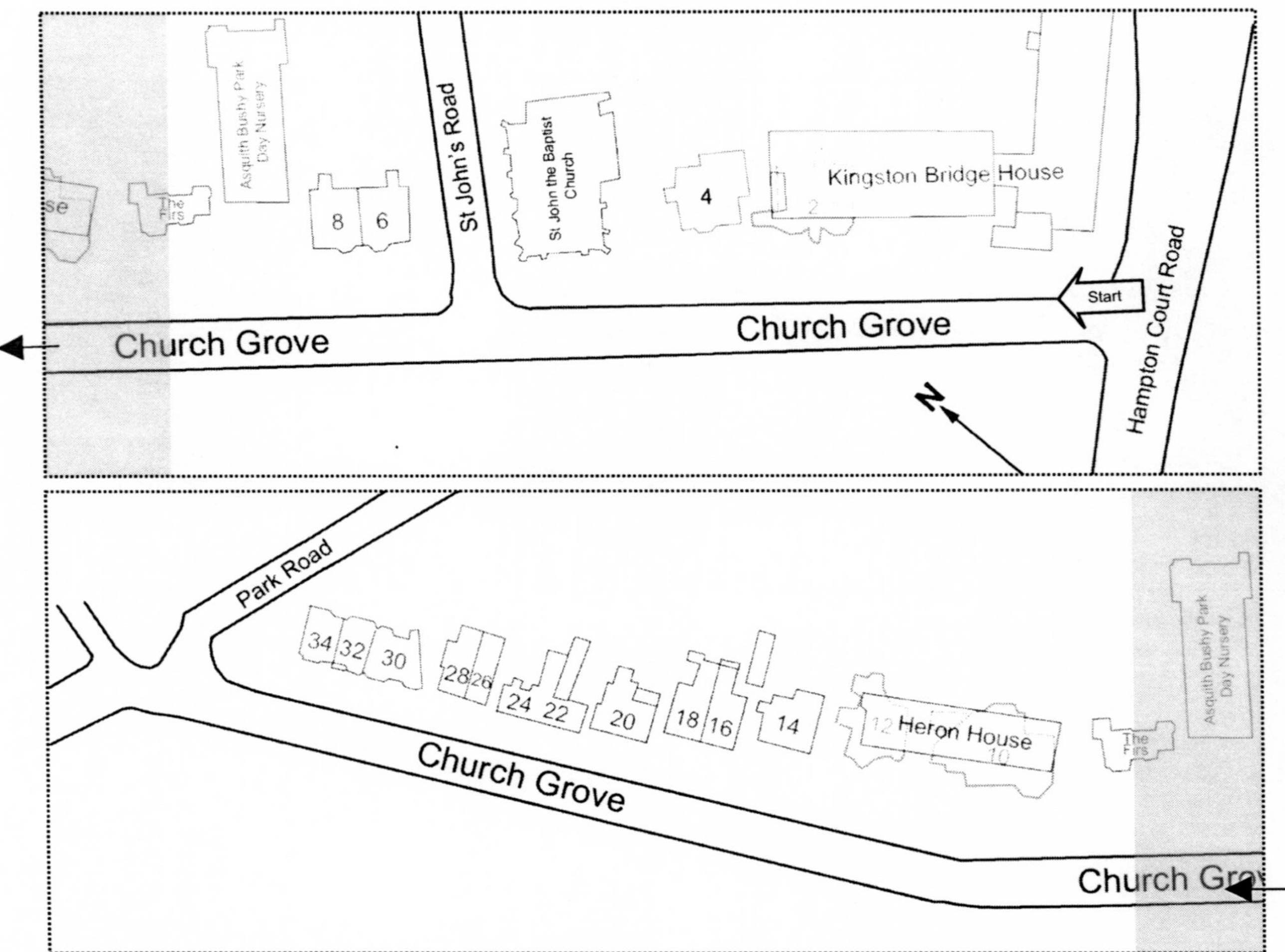
Asquith Bushy Park Day Nursery
The Firs
8
6
St John's Road
St John the Baptist Church
4
Kingston Bridge House
Start
Church Grove
Church Grove
Hampton Court Road
N
Park Road
34
32
30
28
26
24
22
20
18
16
14
12
Heron House
10
The Firs
Asquith Bushy Park Day Nursery
Church Grove
Church Gro

CHURCH GROVE

Brick by Brick

Church Grove was the first new road to be built in Hampton Wick in the timespan covered by this book. It was created in 1824 by order of The Crown as a condition of sale of the land at the south-east corner of Bushy Park (see page 17). The purchaser was Edward Lapidge who was commissioned to build the chapel (later church) of *St John the Baptist* on land he himself donated. Although this building was completed in 1830, no further construction took place until the late 1840s. Its position overlooking the Park made Church Grove a natural location for building large mansions. Known simply as "The New Road" until 1860, it was then called Park Grove until the Local Board's decision in 1863 to rename it Church Grove. This change was unpopular with several residents, one of whom removed the newly-erected road-signs in the dead of night. As elsewhere in the village, some of the large houses were bought up by developers in the 1960s as sites for higher rise schemes such as *Kingston Bridge House* and *Heron House*. Today's Church Grove, with its mixture of original and new properties, retains much of the original character although the heavy pollarding of the street trees contrasts markedly with the luxuriant canopies in the old postcard views (see next page).

CHURCH GROVE
N.AMPTON WICH

4

Opposite page top to bottom:

Kingston Bridge House erected in 1960 was the first purpose-built office block in Hampton Wick. It was refurbished in 1995 and now provides accommodation for 200 Kingston University students.

Church Grove postcard view from around 1915 (middle)

Fairlight (bottom) was built in 1850 by Edward Lapidge as a Vicarage for the next door church, but was never used as such.

this page, top and bottom:

The Church of St John the Baptist built by Edward Lapidge and completed in 1830 **[55]**

Park Villa/The Nest (below), built in 1873 by Henry Wheeler **[79]**

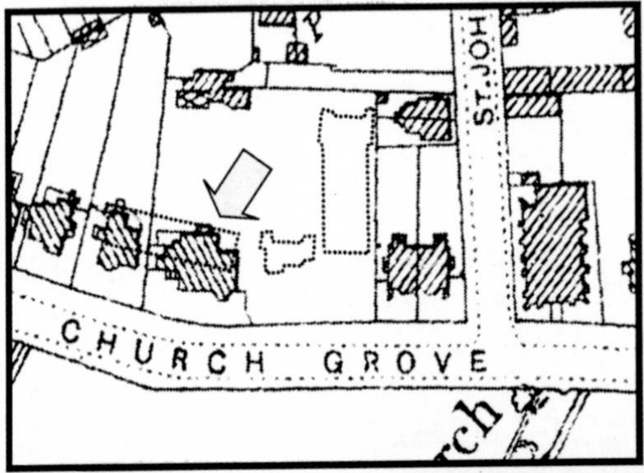
ST. JOH
CHURCH GROVE
rch

Opposite page: These two properties were built on land once belonging to the original Number 10 known as *The Limes* - shown arrowed on the map section (centre).

Ronayne Hall (top) was built in 1928 as the church hall and named after the serving Vicar. It was an important meeting venue and was used for a variety of functions from tombolas, whist drives, and scout/guide meetings to - as the commemorative plaque on the gateposts records - meetings of the Temperance Society. In recent years, the Church sold the hall and it is now used as a day nursery.

The Firs (bottom) was built in 1925.

this page: *The Limes* itself, together with *Bay Villa* at Number 12, were demolished in 1965 to make way for *Heron House* (above), a development containing 21 flats. Each flat was provided with its own lock-up garage behind the property but the Developer retained ownership of these and, after a lengthy dispute over rights of way with the *Heron House* Resident's Association, has recently demolished and replaced them with *Heron Mews* containing three properties.

14
R

R
18
16

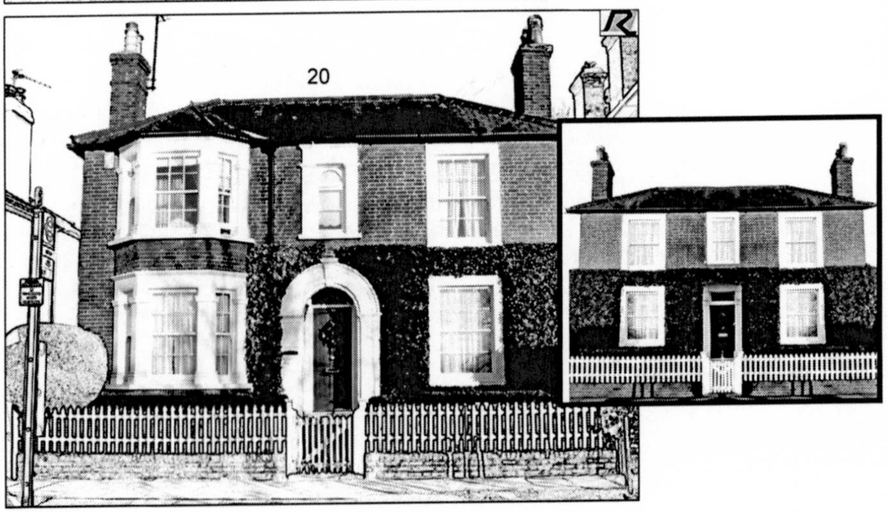
R
20

Opposite page: *Suffolk Lodge* Number 14 Church Grove (top) was built in 1855 by Henry Ryley Wilson. Like many other buildings of its vintage, this has now been converted into six flats. However, as the 1900s snapshot (inset) shows, the once-elegant roofline was lost in conversion.

1 and 2 *Victoria Villas* aka 16 and 18 Church Grove (middle) were built in 1852, again (like *Suffolk Lodge*) by Henry Ryley Wilson but unlike this neighbour these two eight-room properties are each still in single occupation.

Hope Cottage Number 20 Church Grove (bottom) was built in 1850 and yet looks - with its two-storey canted bay and round-arched porch - to be unmistakably late-Victorian. The answer is to be found in an amazing 1901 planning application that shows the whole of the north wall (and chimney) was extended outwards by 70 cms, the bay added and the porch remodelled. Air-brushing away these later additions (inset) reveals a typical, handsome 1850's facade matching many of its Park Road contemporaries **[66]**.

this page: 1 and 2 *Betley Villas* 22/24 Church Grove was the first secular building (1849) to be constructed on this road. It was the work of James Sabine **[61]** who hailed from Titchfield in Hampshire so why he should name his property after a small village in Staffordshire is unclear. The layout is unusual in that, although the houses are semi-detached, they each have a central door and hallway. The simple, elegant facade is covered in stucco, rusticated on the lower storey to imitate separate blocks of stone. The external porches with their tented canopies are sublime - adding to the appearance of what is surely one of the most attractive properties in Hampton Wick.

These five properties - **Numbers 26/28** (above) and **30 to 34** (opposite right top to bottom) - at the end of Church Grove were all built by Christopher Wren. The marked dissimilarity between these buildings and, say, Hampton Court Palace is explained by the fact that this particular Christopher Wren was born in Kingston upon Thames in 1871. He was the landlord at the *Grove Inn* (now *Navigator House*) when he bought the land. It had once been the gardens of Numbers 38 and 40 Park Road (below left and, arrowed, right). On it he built he built his two sets of houses: Numbers 26/28 in 1910 and Numbers 30-34 in 1920. He called these latter (seen under construction in 1920 opposite, bottom) ***Flemish Villas*** after his great passion for rabbit breeding, especially the giant Flemish breed (opposite, top left).

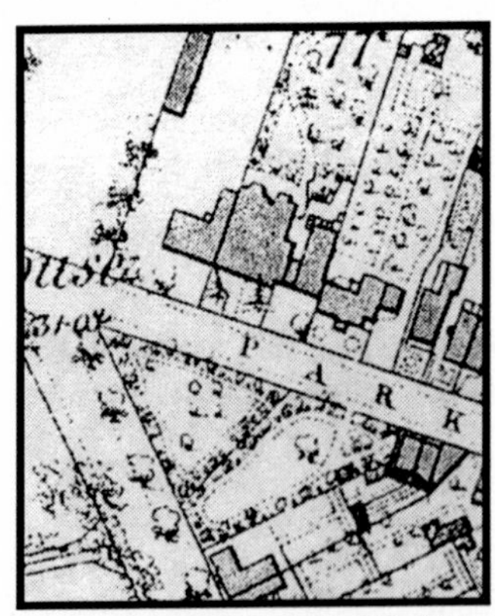

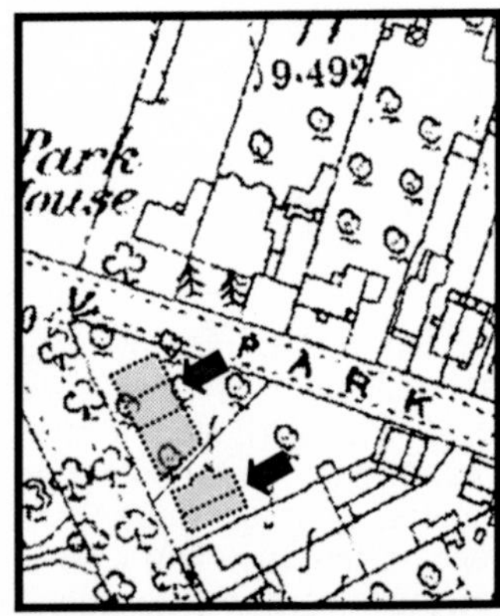

Above
Christopher Wren bought the plot laying in the corner between Park Road and Church Grove which had been part of the gardens of *Park House* and *Green Cottage*.

30

32

34
32
30

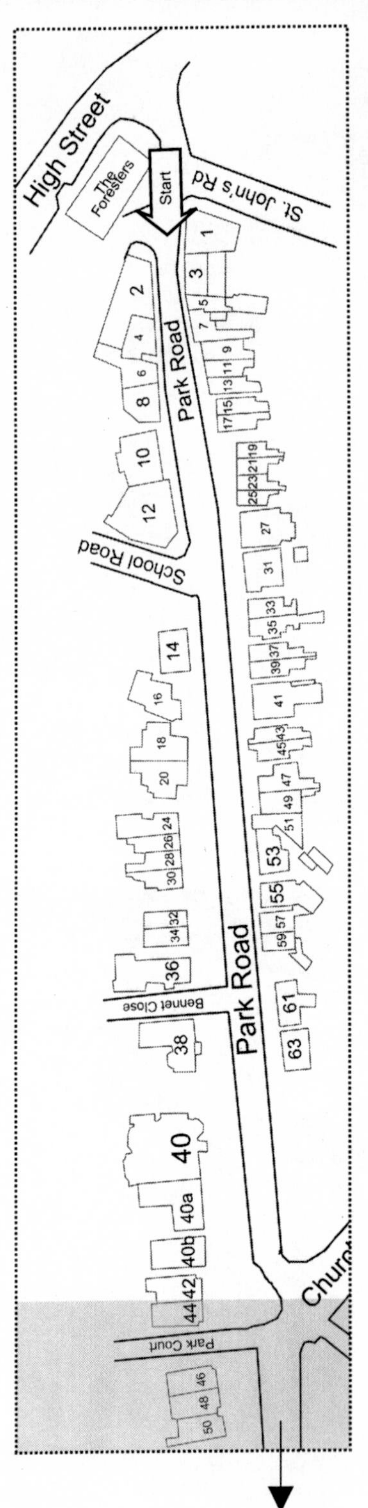

High Street
The Foresters
Start
St. John's Rd
Park Road
School Road
Bennet Close
Park Road
Church
Park Court

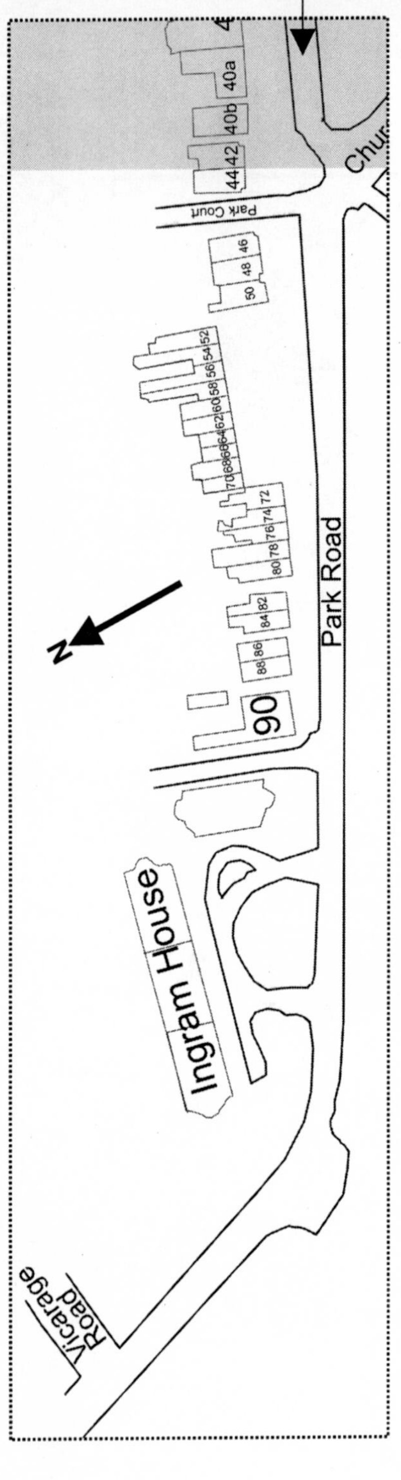

Park Court
Church
N
Park Road
Ingram House
Vicarage Road

PARK ROAD

Brick by Brick

Park Road is the start of the route from Hampton Wick to Hounslow Heath and appears on the very earliest maps of the locality. It commences from the end of St John's Road opposite *The Foresters* and runs straight in a west north westerly direction. After 240 metres it meets Church Grove and the park boundary wall which it then skirts for 300 metres, ending just before it reaches the Timothy Bennet Memorial and the pedestrian gate into Bushy Park. At this point the road turns in a more northerly direction and continues as Sandy Lane. Earlier known simply and prosaically as "the road leading to Bushy-park", it was officially named Park Road by the Local Board in 1863.

The earliest buildings - as seen on the eighteenth century maps - were at the southern end along with *The Cedars* and its estate and two market gardens towards the north-western end. The first new developments took place on the north-eastern side of the road starting in 1830 and it was not until the 1850s that the south-western side was developed with 26 properties constructed between the junctions with St John's Road and Church Grove during the decade.

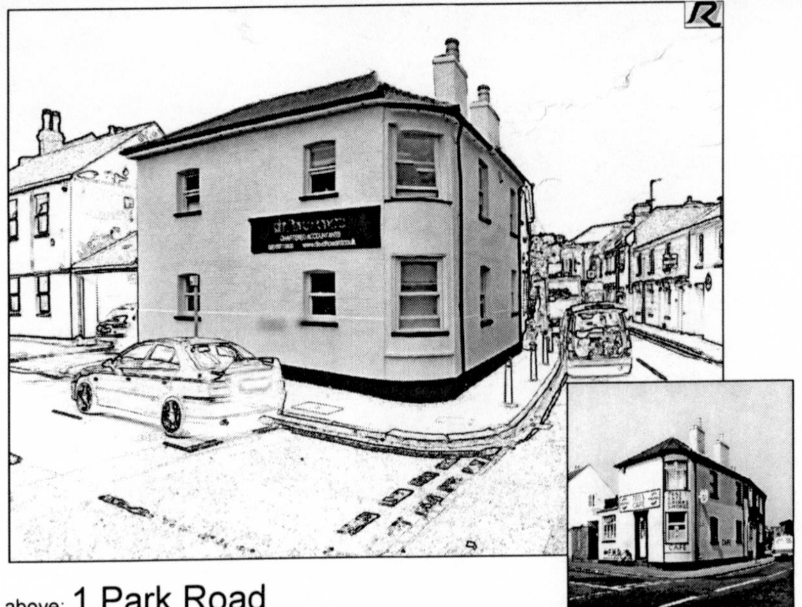

above: **1 Park Road**

Built in 1850 by Robert Belchamber who was running his building business from the yard next door in St John's Road. In 1861 he opened Number 1 as the "*Prince of Wales Beer Tavern*". By 1904 it was a coffee tavern (below) and then a cafe up until the 1970s (inset above right). It finally became an office building in 1994.

below: **Park Road around 1910**

This view was taken by Richard Young of Teddington. Remarkably little has changed architecturally apart from the Dutch Gables added to *The Foresters* in the 1930s. The Victoria Jubilee Fountain was moved from this position to permit road widening in the 1920s. The *Assembly Rooms* are clearly visible in the distance.

above: **2 Park Road**

Built around 1860 by Charles Miles who lived at 35 Park Road. From the outset it was leased out as a grocer's shop with a wine and spirits licence and continued in this trade until converted into a private house around 1971.

below: **2 Park Road around 1970**

Many of today's residents still remember Mae Smith and her off-licence. The two shop fronts have disappeared and replaced by conventional but non-period windows. Notice the Public Conveniences in the basement of the Council Offices. Though long since closed, the facilities are still in place.

above: 3 Park Road

Numbers 3 and 5 were built around 1851 by Robert Belchamber as an extension to his property at Number 1. Belchamber died in 1876 by which time Number 5 had probably already been split off. Number 3 appears to have become a separate property around 1879.

below: 5 Park Road

above: 4 Park Road
Probably originally part of Number 2, this five-room property has been a separate entity since at least the time of the 1891 Census.

below: *1 and 2 Rose Cottages,* 6-8 Park Road
Built around 1885 by Sir Thomas James Nelson, who was the then chairman of the Local Board. It was under his leadership that the redevelopment scheme for this part of Park Road was planned and executed **[83]** and some in the village accused him of having a conflict of interests.

left 7 Park Road

Built in the 1850s by William Worrall who was a solicitor's managing clerk. The 1911 Census recorded the house as having four-rooms although recent sales particulars showing six-rooms suggest it has since been extended at the back.

left *Avondale Cottages*

9-13 Park Road

Number 9-11 were built in the early 1850s by John Beauchamp whose father ran the dairy located at 14 Park Road. Beside helping his father, John Junior was also a pork butcher and added a shop at Number 13 – the wide lintel shows where the former shop-front had been located and notice how the brickwork is not keyed into Number 11.

left *Myrtle Cottages*

15/17 Park Road

Built in the 1850s.

Major Redevelopment of 6-12 Park Road in the 1880s

Some of the worst housing in Hampton Wick lay between the High Street and Park Road - shown as the cross-hatched area on the 1863 section of the map collage below. These included an old area known as *The Pits* - an apposite description in modern parlance but probably more associated with the Old English word "pytt" meaning water hole (there was a pond nearby). A second area was known as *Ayling Place* named after the builder who created them. Together these were a set of 16 miserable wooden dwellings and the descriptions of their conditions, especially the sanitary arrangements, make uncomfortable reading.

The Local Board first targetted these dwellings for slum clearance as early as 1864 but it was not until the 1880s that they had the electoral confidence - in the face of an uncertain community mandate - to demolish them. The ground thus released provided the site for a much-needed extension to the Girls and Infants National School as well the new Local Board offices. It also gave rise to the new School Road - and the renaming of an existing and very old thoroughfare, School Lane.

Ayling Place became *Mayfield* (Number 10) - now the Chase Lodge Hotel - and the *Assembly Rooms* at Number 12 - now Kellys Dance Studio. Further east the new properties were called *Rose Cottages* at Numbers 6/8 Park Road.

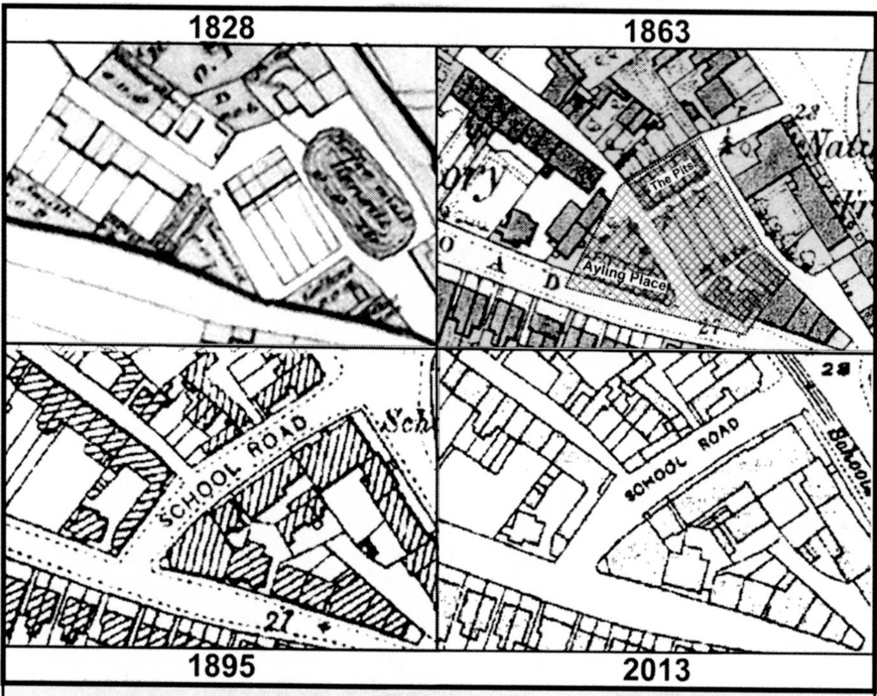

above: The area on which School Road was eventually built contained some of the worst slums in Hampton Wick, notably the areas known as The *Pits* and *Ayling Place*, marked and shown cross-hatched in the 1863 section of this map collage.

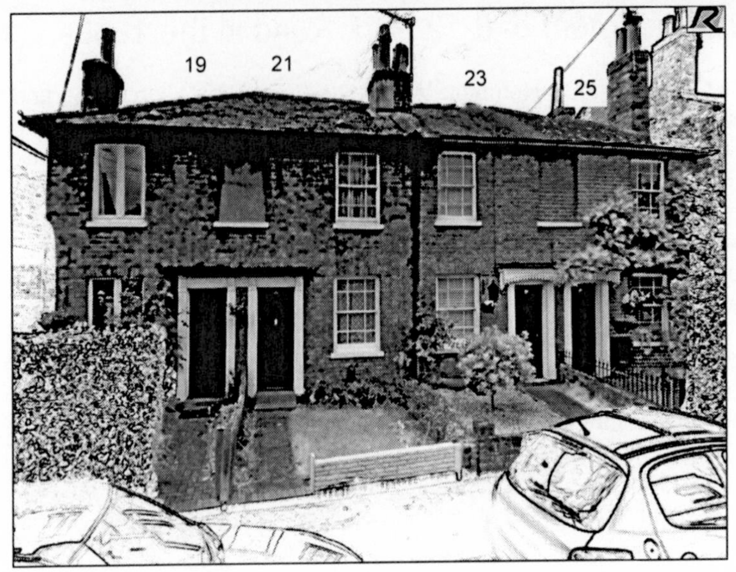

above

Beaumont Cottages

19-25 Park Road

Built around 1850 by Edward Alfred Wright **[68]** and named after his wife Sarah Beaumont James.

left ***Laurel Cottage***

27/29 Park Road

Two four-room semi-detached cottages (one with a rear entrance) built around 1858 by John Wright **[68]**, brother of Edward.

left ***Meadow Cottage***

31 Park Road

This beautiful eight-room property was built in 1850 by Edward Albert Wright as his own home.

above: *Mayfield* , 10 Park Road

Built in 1888 following the demolition of *The Pits* and the creation of School Road **[83]**. For many years, the Ayliffe family lived here, whilst running their coal yard which was on School Lane. The building became a hotel in the 1980s.

below: *The Assembly Rooms*, 12 Park Road

Opened in 1887, the lease was originally held by the Hampton Wick Local Board and has only recently been sold to the current tenant by the London Borough of Richmond upon Thames. The building was used as a venue for dancing from the outset and has been a dedicated dance studio since 1928. The main studio (seen inset around 1940) still seems to retain many original features.

Source: Keith and Kornelia Kelly

above *Alpha Cottages*
33/35 Park Road
and …

left *Cecilia Cottages*
37/39 Park Road

These two pairs of four-roomed cottages were built by Alfred Wright - father of Edward and John - around 1850. They were given to his daughters Emma and Cecilia respectively who sublet them to Jesse Huntingford in 1859.

left 41 Park Road

Another beautiful property built in 1850 this time by Jesse Huntingford **[68]** for his daughter and son-in-law William Lindsey. Jesse himself lived here from 1859 until his death in 1879.

above: *The Dairy,* 14 Park Road

A dairy has stood on this site from at least the late eighteenth century when Daniel and later John Beauchamp were the dairyman tenants. The Beauchamps continued until 1890 when George Smith and his sons took over the business. The present house probably dates from around 1858.

below: 16 Park Road

Built in 2002 after the original planning refusal was reversed on appeal.

left *Clare Cottages* 43/45 Park Road

A pair of five-roomed cottages built by Jesse Huntingford in 1850. Note the blind window which features in almost all houses built by Huntingford and Wright on Park Road.

above *Albion Cottages and Albion House* 47/49 and 51 Park Road

The cottages were built around 1850 by Thomas Dale. He added the house around 1861. Despite the narrow frontage, the house had five-rooms due to its unusual fan-shaped plot.. (inset)

left *Ivy Cottage* 53 Park Road

Built by James Sabine in 1850.

above: **18/20 Park Road**
Built 1991 by Simon Arch.

below: ***The Priory,* 24-32 Park Road**
Built around 1830 by William Walton. This unusual Grade 2 Listed building was built in the Strawberry Hill Gothick style pioneered by Horace Walpole at his nearby confection **[54].** In its original format, the outer two houses had five-rooms each with the centre two having four.

left *Ravensholme*

55 Park Road

Built in 1891 in the garden of *Ivy Cottage*. The single-storey bay window and heavily perforated barge boards on the gable end look surprisingly out of place in this predominantly early-Victorian street.

above left

Clarence Cottages
57/59 Park Road

The cottages were built around 1850 by George Constable. Like their immediate neighbours, these properties have unusual fan-shaped plots which brings the building line forward to the pavement.

above and left

61 and 63 Park Road

Built in 1932 and 1986 (the latter by Jim Sheridan) in the rear gardens of 26-34 Church Grove.

above ***Oak Villa***

32/34 Park Road

This pair of semi-detached houses were built around 1830 by the same William Walton who created the extravaganza that is *The Priory* next door. *Oak Villa* is a much more restrained design which befitted its role as a Young Ladies' Academy which was run for almost 40 years by Miss Mary Slow **[51]**.

Left and below ***Virginia Lodge***

36 Park Road

Built by 1850 by John Walker, proprietor of Number 38, in the corner of his garden. The photograph from the 1930s (below) shows the narrow entrance to the brass foundry on the site of today's Library.

left *Green Cottage*

38 Park Road

Built in 1830 by Henry Walker. The footprint has changed over the years [**49**], most recently being reduced on the southern side to accommodate the entrance to Bennet Close.

left

Park House

40 Park Road

Built in 1830 by George Ferriman for Charles James Fenner who ran Fenner's Academy here for 40 years **[40]**. The property used to incorporate all the land now occupied by *Park Court* behind as well as the triangle of land opposite between Park Road and Church Grove.

left

40a Park Road

Probably built at the same time as the main house, this block may have provided the classroom for the Academy. The three tall windows and the high ceiling would be in keeping.

left

40b Park Road

The coach house and stables were built sometime between 1880 and 1895.

above:
This panorama of the rear of *Park House* Numbers 40-40b shows both the scale of the total property and the elegance with which 40a and 40b have been remodelled.

Below:
A postcard view of this end of Park Road taken around 1910. The wall on the extreme right encloses the orchard belonging to *Park House*.

Above left to right: **50-46 and 44/42 Park Road**
Built 1922.
Below:
The entrance to *Park Court*. For several years this roadway was used by lorries removing sand and ballast from the quarrying operations behind.

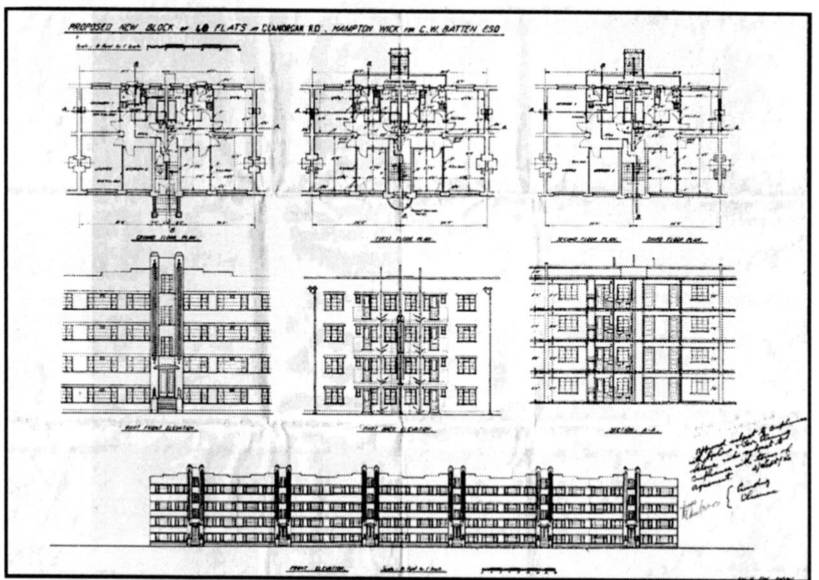

Park Court

A development of three four-storey blocks containing a total of 72 flats were built 1936-38 on the land originally belonging to *Park House*.

top The plans as approved by the Local Council when the development was originally intended for Glamorgan Road. The stepped parapets emphasis the entrance halls.

right
This detail from the OS map shows how the three blocks are located at the edges of the site to ensure firm foundations: the centre had been used as a quarry.

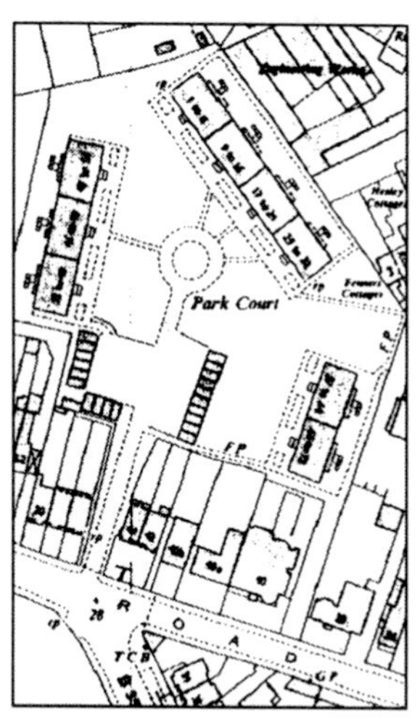

52

56
54

58

Opposite page top to bottom

1, 2 and 3, 4 Park View Cottages,

52-58 Park Road

Built 1849 by John Reed **[62]**.

This page, right to left, to and middle

6, 5 and 4, 3, 2 and 1 Park Row

60-70 Park Road

Built around 1835 by John Reed **[62]**

above: *Reeds Cottages*

This postcard view from around 1910 shows the six *Park Row Cottages* (nearest the camera) and the four *Park View Cottages* beyond. All were built by John Reed in 1837 and 1849 respectively.

below: 1-3 *Spring Grove Cottages*, 72-76 Park Road

Built in 1858 by William Salter Minchin who, with his mother Sarah, ran the nearby Nursery Ground.

above: *Park Hatch*, 78/80 Park Road
Built in 1896 by Alfred Huntingford on land which had previously provided access to *Garden Cottages* behind, which he also owned. These latter were displaced by Vineyard Row (1970s) but a vestige of the original access remains beside Number 80.

below: *Park End Cottages*, 82/84 Park Road
Built in 1858.

above: *Norfolk Cottage and Park Cottage*, 86/88 Park Road

Built in 1859 by Charles Worsfield, a master blacksmith who had his forge on the High Street.

below: *Park End House*, 90 Park Road

The original house on this site was built around 1808 by Samuel Hampton. The present structure by Robert Sivers dates from 1879 though whether as a remodelling of the earlier design or as a complete rebuild is unclear.

above: *Ingram House*
Built in 1936, the main block has 24 flats with a further eight flats in the smaller block to the south. There is also a separate caretaker's house.

below: *The Old Vicarage*
Built in 1855/6 by the Lord Chancellor for use by the Vicar of St John the Baptist, this photograph was probably taken shortly before this 11-room Victorian Gothic mansion was demolished in 1935 to make way for *Ingram House*.

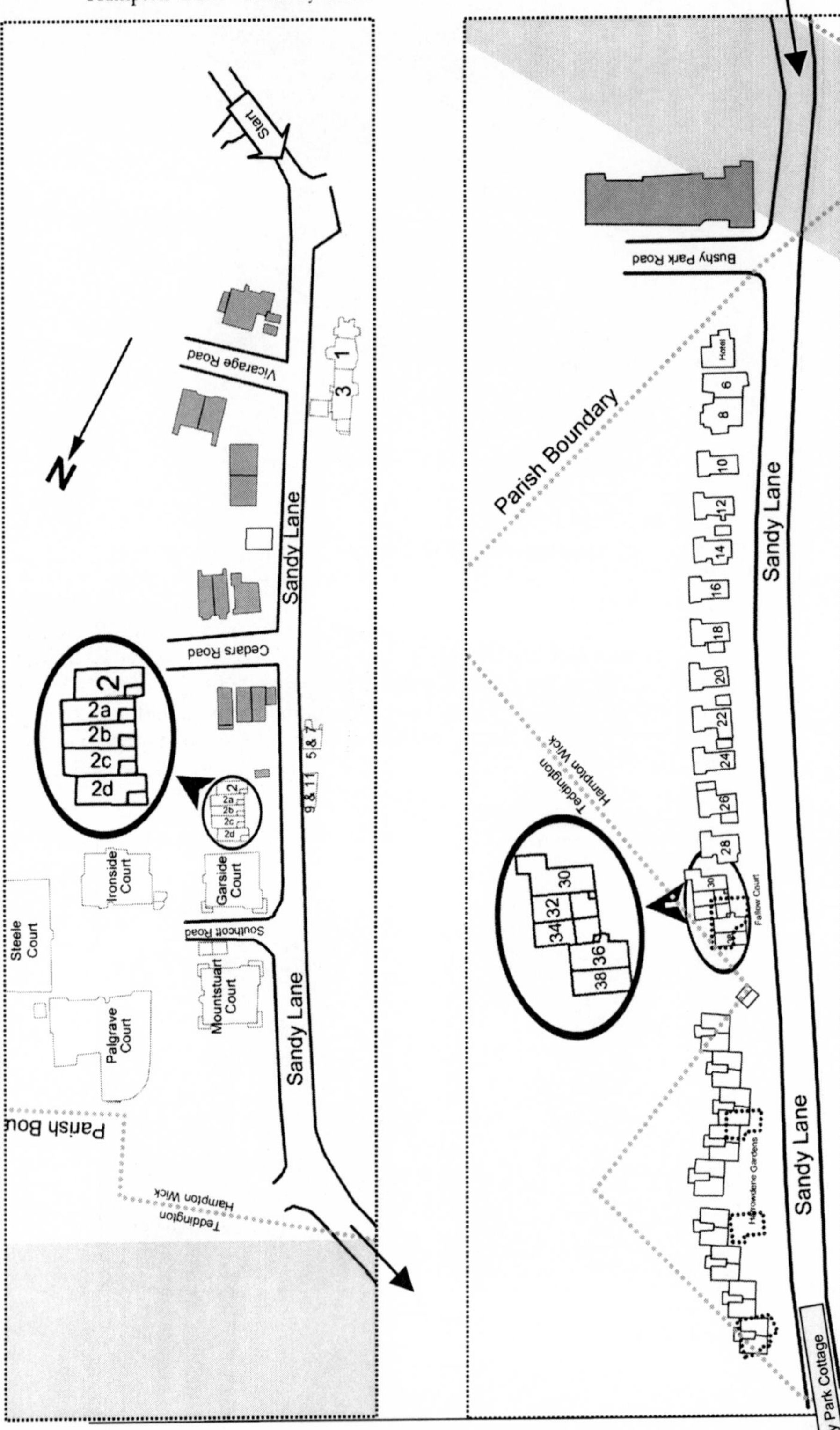
Start
N
Vicarage Road
Sandy Lane
Cedars Road
Southcott Road
1
3
5 & 7
9 & 11
2
2a
2b
2c
2d
Garside Court
Ironside Court
Steele Court
Mountstuart Court
Palgrave Court
Parish Bou
Teddington
Hampton Wick
Bushy Park Road
Parish Boundary
Hotel
6
8
10
12
14
16
18
20
22
24
26
28
30
32
34
36
38
Fallow Court
Harrowdene Gardens
To Bushy Park Cottage

SANDY LANE

Brick by Brick

Sandy Lane runs from the end of Park Road to where the parish boundary crosses it for the third and final time at *Harrowdene Gardens.* This thoroughfare owes its existence to King Henry VIII. When the King, who already owned Hampton Court Palace (courtesy of Cardinal Wolsey), acquired the neighbouring Manor of Teddington, he was able to enlarge Bushy Park to give himself more space to enjoy his passion for stag-hunting. So, whereas Park Road previously ran in a more or less straight line between Hampton Wick and Teddington gates, it was now diverted round the wall of the expanded park on a route which was first known as the New Road and later became Sandy Lane.

Being on the boundary, Sandy Lane was frequently the subject of quarrels between the authorities in Hampton Wick and Teddington, each accusing the other of failing to maintain the highway in a fit state.

1/3

9
13
7
11

Opposite top left **The Hampton Wick Gate and the Timothy Bennet Memorial**

The story of a cobbler who took on the Earl of Halifax, won his case in the courts, and provided the public with a path through the Park forever.

Opposite middle ***The Thatched House*** **1/3 Sandy Lane**

Built in the early 1830s using the Cottage Orné style, this property has recently been faithfully restored **[35]**.

Opposite bottom: ***Sandy Lane Cottages*****, 5-11 Sandy Lane**

The original stables and coach house were converted around 1908 to provide four 4-room flats.

Below, clockwise from top right ***Liberty House*** **, Numbers 2 and 2a-2d Sandy Lane**

The four-bedroomed *Liberty House* has recently been built in the garden of Number 47 Cedars Road as part of the redevelopment of that site. Number 2 is a semi-detached house and 2a-2d are townhouses built in 1985 on the site of Cedars House which British Gas acquired as part of the 1948 nationalisation of the Gas Industry.

above: **Linden Homes Phase 1 Sandy Lane**

The redevelopment of the original gasworks site **[120]** was a local *cause célèbre*. Permission was finally given in July 2006. The first phase consists of these four 4-storey blocks and a crèche.

below: ***Bushy Park Lodge*, Sandy Lane**

Given the vagaries of the Hampton Wick boundary at this point, Phase 2 of the Linden Homes is actually wholly within Teddington. Bushy Park Lodge, designed by Richard Pain, was built right up to the boundary around 2000: note how the south-east wall of the car park is aligned at 45 degrees following the boundary line.

Opposite **Numbers 6 to 28 Sandy Lane**

Henry Spinks built these 12 "identical" houses around 1900. Each had seven-rooms and was centred on its generously wide plot. Over the years owners and developers have created such a variety of projects that it is sometimes difficult to identify the original structure.

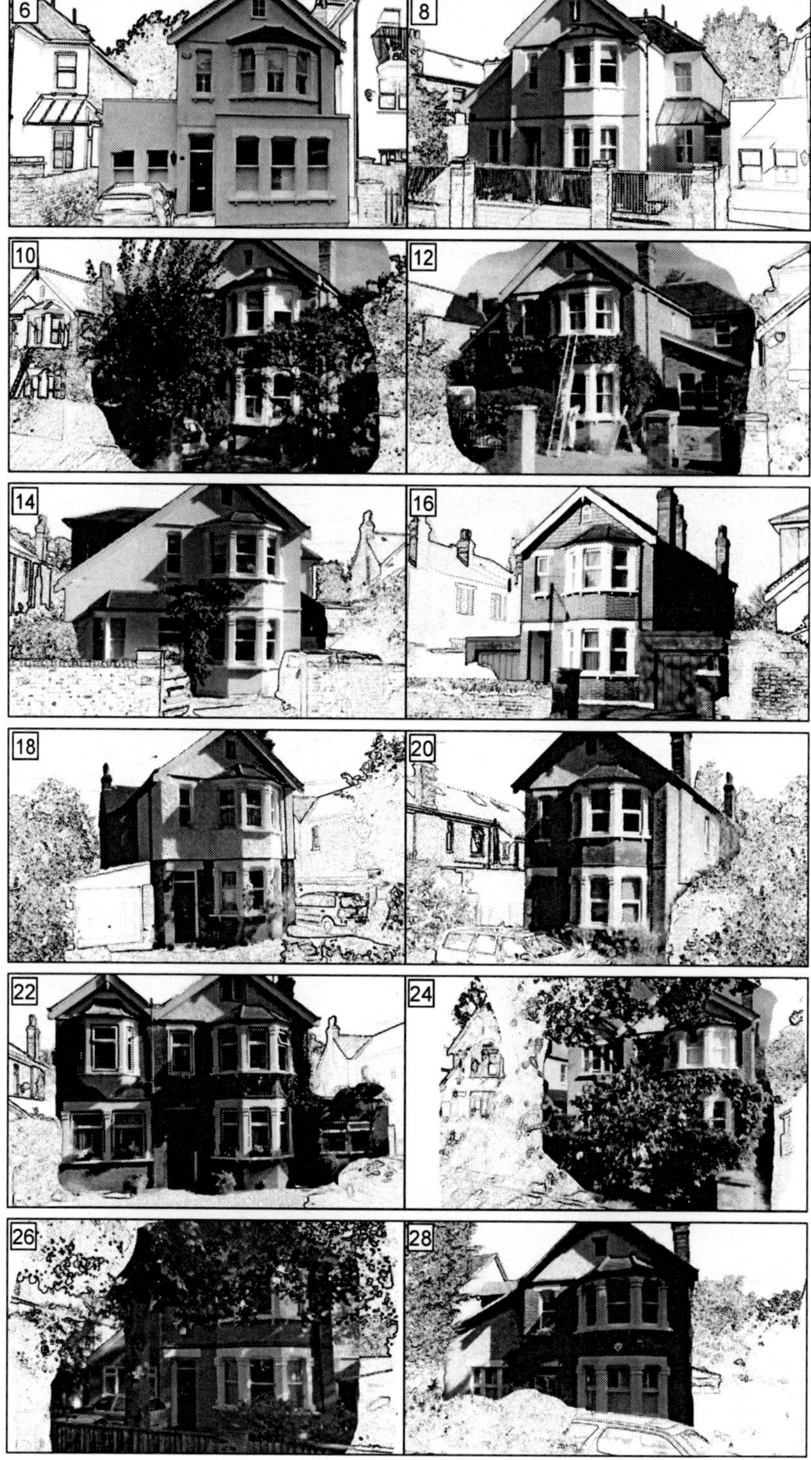
6
8
10
12
14
16
18
20
22
24
26
28

above: *Fallow Court* 30-38 Sandy Lane
A development of five three-storey town houses built in 1989.

below: *Harrowdene Gardens*, Sandy Lane
Built in 1967 by Wates on former wartime railway sidings. The total estate comprises 132 properties but only the few fronting onto Sandy Lane are within Hampton Wick.

Above and below: *Bushy Park Cottage*

Queen's Road, Teddington

700 metres beyond the "end" of Hampton Wick, at the junction of Queen's and Park Roads, lies this beautiful property in a detached part of the parish. Built in the late eighteenth century, the building was the official Parsonage House for Hampton Wick from 1835-1858 hence (probably) its inclusion within in the official parish.

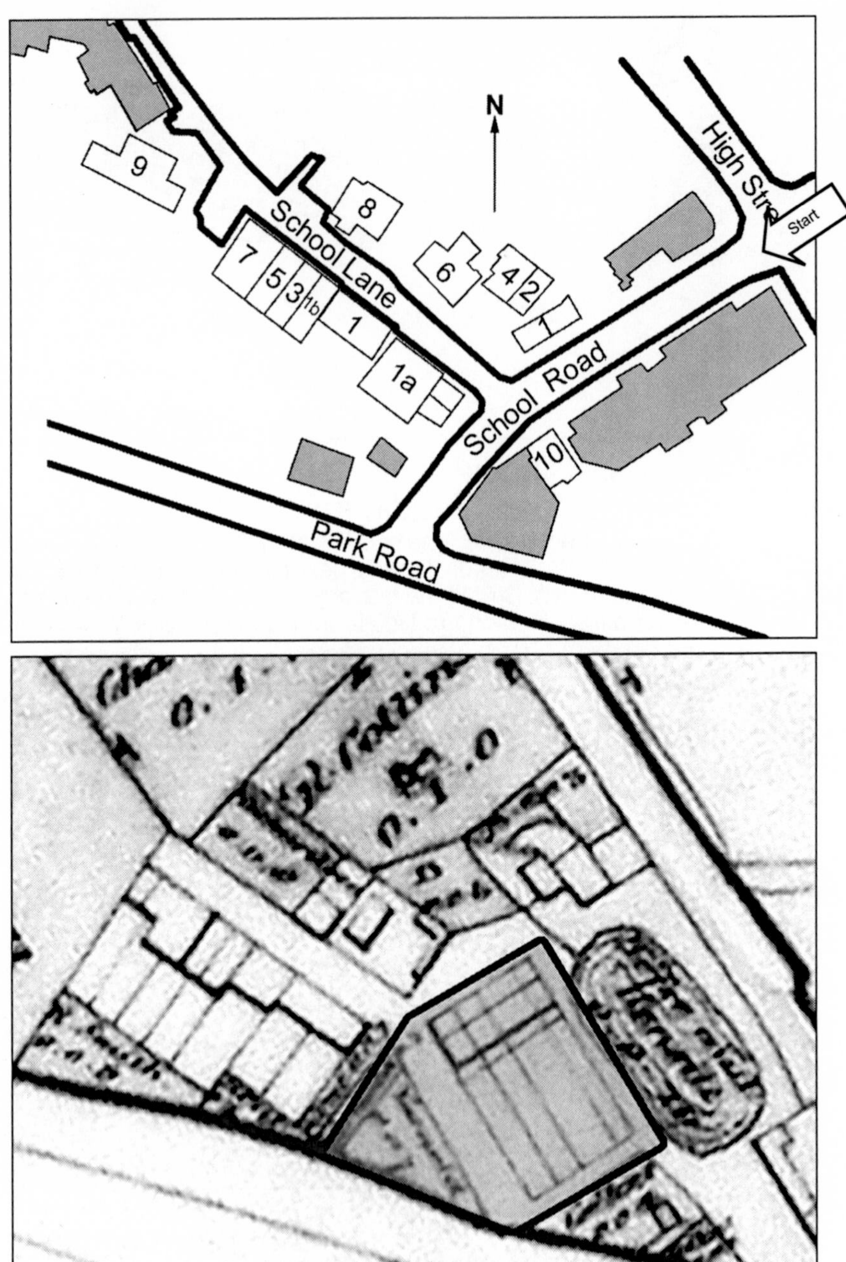
N
9
8
School Lane
7
5
3
1b
1
1a
6
4
2
1
School Road
10
Park Road
Start

SCHOOL LANE

SCHOOL ROAD

Brick by Brick

School Lane is one of the oldest thoroughfares in Hampton Wick and gave access to a large number of poor quality working-class tenements. By contrast, School Road was built in 1886 precisely for the purpose of clearing some of those slums (indicated in grey on the lower map opposite which dates from 1828). The full story is told on page 83. The streets owed their name to the fact that the new extensions for the Girls and Infants School were built on the south-east side of the new road (now the site of *Brentham House*). School Road has only two properties accessed from it whereas the similar length School Lane has eleven.

Brentham House

Girls' and Infants' School

10

Opposite top and middle: *Brentham House*, 45c High Street
Built in the 1970s on the site of the Girls' and Infants' School (lower photograph - courtesy of Paul Barnfield). The underground car park is at the level of the original school playground.

Opposite bottom: 10 School Road
Built in 1889 as part of the Assembly Room buildings, it was used as staff accommodation. Recently it was sold by its owner, the London Borough of Richmond upon Thames, and is now part of the Chase Lodge Hotel.

This page, top: *Sunnyside,* 1 School Road
Built in 1887 by Silvester Smith Towell, a local builder who retired and spent his last years in this house. The building has a full-width basement.

top and left:

1c and 1b School Lane

Built around 1981 by Simon Arch on land that was part of the garden of 14 Park Road.

bottom: **1a School Lane**

This property first appeared as a separate entity around 1920 when it presumably was built or converted from part of Number 1.

top and left:

2 and 4 School Lane

Built sometime before 1863.

bottom: **6 School Lane**

The previous property on this site was demolished around 1940 but its replacement, though approved, was never built. The current building dates from the early 1980s and has access from both School Lane and School Road.

1
3
5
7

9

Opposite top and bottom left:

1-4 *Walker's Cottages*, 1-7 School Lane

Probably the oldest properties on this side of the village, this row of cottages is shown on the 1828 map, at which time their back gardens ran down to Park Road. The footprints remained unchanged until they were redeveloped in the early 1990's by Simon Arch.

Opposite bottom right:

9 School Road

This bungalow was built in 1993 for his parents by Simon Arch who had previously used the land as a builder's yard.

This page, top:

10 School Road

Built in 1991 on the site of the coal yard operated by the Ayliffe family for many years.

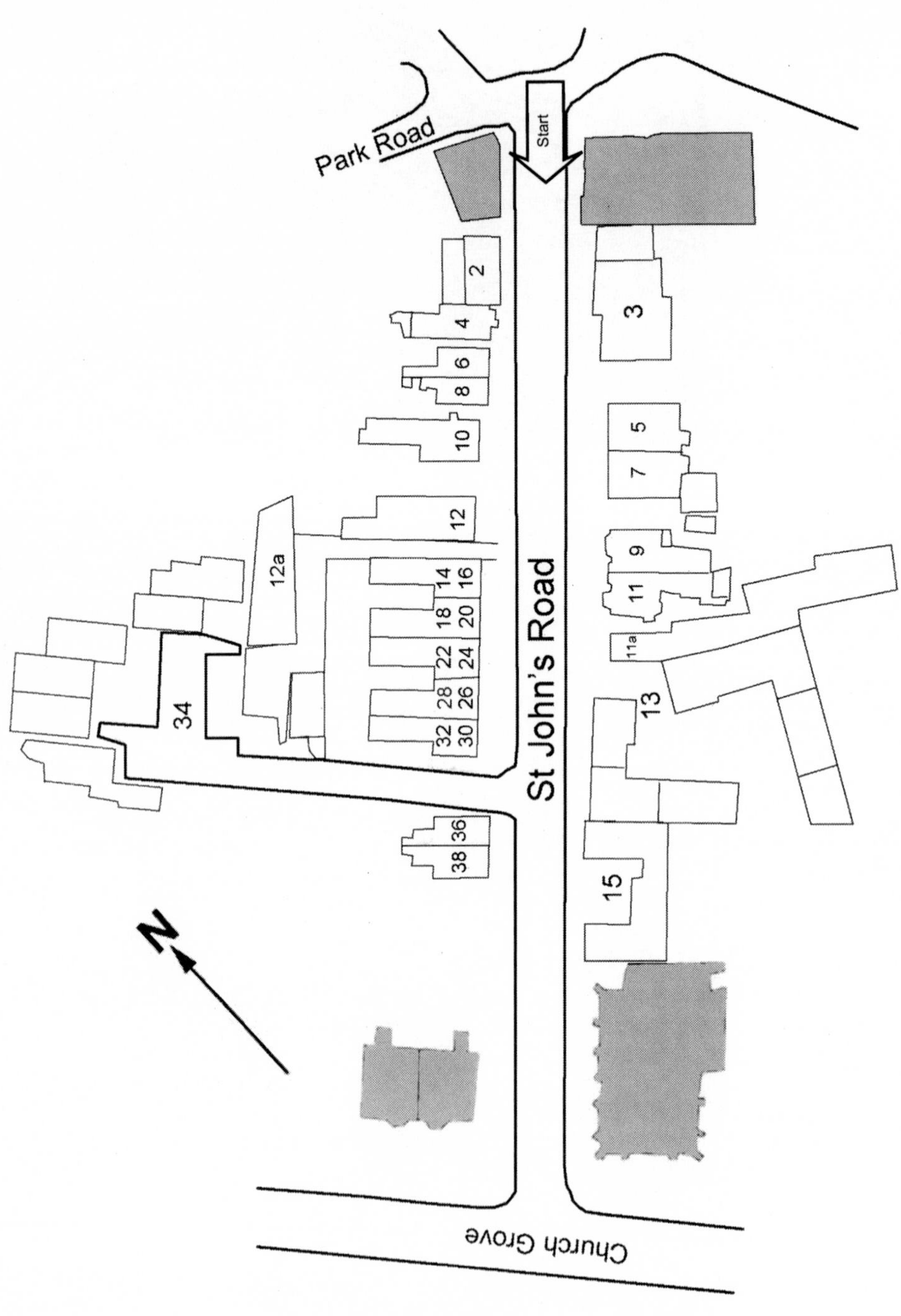
Park Road
Start
St John's Road
Church Grove
N
2
3
4
6
8
5
7
10
12
9
11
12a
14
16
18
20
22
24
28
26
32
30
34
11a
13
36
38
15

St JOHN's ROAD

Brick by Brick

St John's Road was laid out by Edward Lapidge in the late 1820's, soon after he had created Church Grove. However, whereas the latter was built in response to the condition placed by The Crown on the land purchase, Lapidge himself needed St John's Road both to provide access to the building plots he had immediately laid out on that land as well as to create a direct route from the centre of the village to the new church he had recently been commissioned to build. There were no immediate takers for his building land until Henry Wheeler purchased the plot opposite the church and built *Grove Cottages* in the late 1850s - the first of several properties the Wheeler family constructed to support their thriving local furniture business. Despite its short length, St John's Road has always played host to a wide range of businesses and residences. Taking 1920 as a datum point, it boasted a brass foundry, a printing works, a furniture factory/warehouse and a coal/corn yard as well as the imposing *de la Pierre Villas* and the row of *Tramway Flats.*

above: 1-3 St John's Road

This mixed development project which totally redeveloped the original St John's Place, includes these 6 flats and was completed in 1982.

below: *de la Pierre Villas,* 5/7 St John's Road

This imposing pair of mid-Victorian semi-detached houses was built in 1864 by John Plow Smith and caused a furore at the Local Board **[77]**. The name derives from Dorothy, Marchioness de la Pierre who owed the original property that stood on this land **[17]**.

opposite, top to bottom:

2, 4 (*Ivernia Cottage*) and 6/8 St John's Road

These properties were respectively built in the 1950s, 1869 (by Charles Bradley) and pre-1863 (by George Constable).

2

4

8
6

above: *Sarnia/Rathmore House* 9/11 St John's Road

Built around 1892 by William Henry Wheeler, this pair of semi-detached houses are unusual in retaining the semi-basement format that was more common in Georgian and early -Victorian properties where large retinues of servants - for whom the basements were built - were more normal.

below: 11a St John's Road

This most unusual design, built around 1996, manages to squeeze a two-bedroom work/live unit (including workshop and studio) onto a tiny plot. As the plan shows, space is saved on all three floors by housing the stairwell within the front semi-circular protrusion.

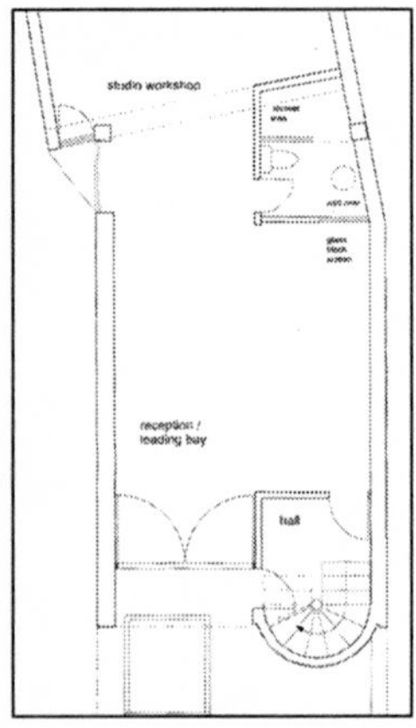

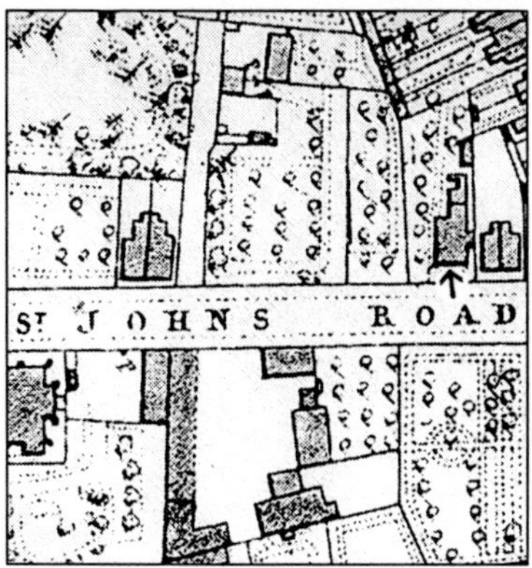

above: *Maude Cottage* 10 St John's Road

Built in 1861 by John William Reed **[62]** and probably named for Colonel Maude who looked after Queen Victoria's royal stud in Bushy Park. Although today's street-facing facade suggests this is a modest-sized property, what we are actually looking at is the original sidewall. The house was built to face *down* the street (see detail from 1863 OS map with the cottage arrowed) and retained its open outlook at the front until the neighbouring land was eventually sold around 1904.

below: *Saxby* 12 St John's Road

A W (Albert) Bullen ran a highly successful gas plumbers' business. He had opened a shop on the corner of Old Bridge Street in 1880 and, by 1897, had built St John's Foundry to manufacture brass fittings for the business. In 1905 he constructed *Saxby* literally beside the factory gates. The following year he closed the High Street shop to concentrate on the foundry operations.

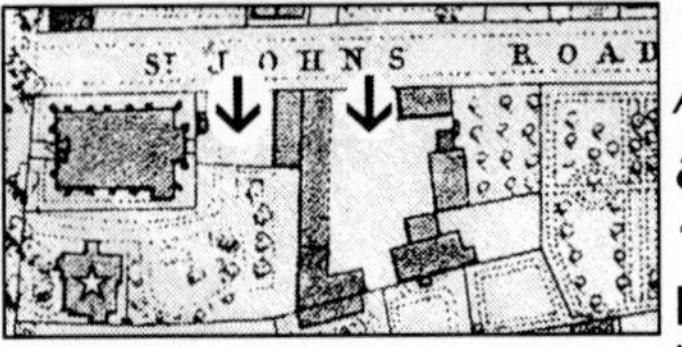

Above and below ***St John's Mews and Fairlight Mews***

13 and 15 St John's Road

Both these live/work developments are located on sites that existed at the time of the 1863 OS map (shown arrowed left), Number 13 being a coal and corn storage yard and Number 15 being the coach house and stable for *Fairlight* (starred). *St John's Mews* is a new build containing seven units and opened around 2004 on the site of the former Eland Engineering (see inset). *Fairlight* Mews is based on the original 1850's buildings. At the time of writing, it is operating as a sound-recording business.

30 32 26 28 22 24 18 20 14 16

Above and left: *Tramway Flats*

14-32 St John's Road

Built in 1904 by London United Tramways Limited to replace one of the High Street tenement blocks demolished to make way for the trams **[102]**. Each of the ten properties are two-bedrooms "half-houses", in that they have their own street entrance (there are two front doors per porchway). Much of the accommodation is in the large rear extension).

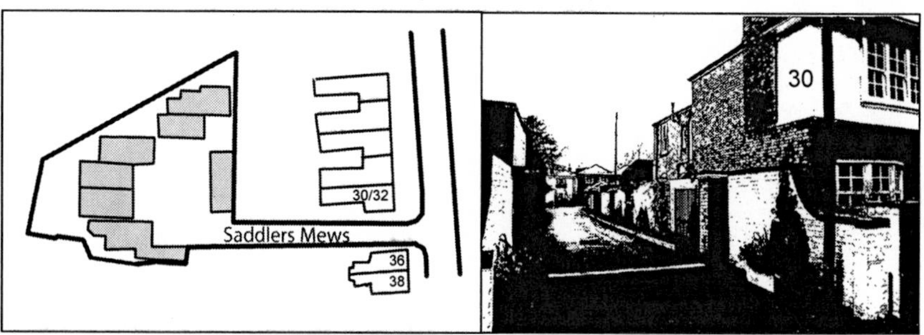

above: *Saddlers Mews* 34 St John's Road

A 1996 development of six properties which incorporates the stable block from the former *The Limes* on Church Grove.

right: *Grove Cottages*

36/38 St John's Road

Built in 1861 by Henry Wheeler to house members of the family involved in his local furniture business **[74]** which ran in its premises next to The Old Kings Head on Hampton Court Road until the mid-1950s.

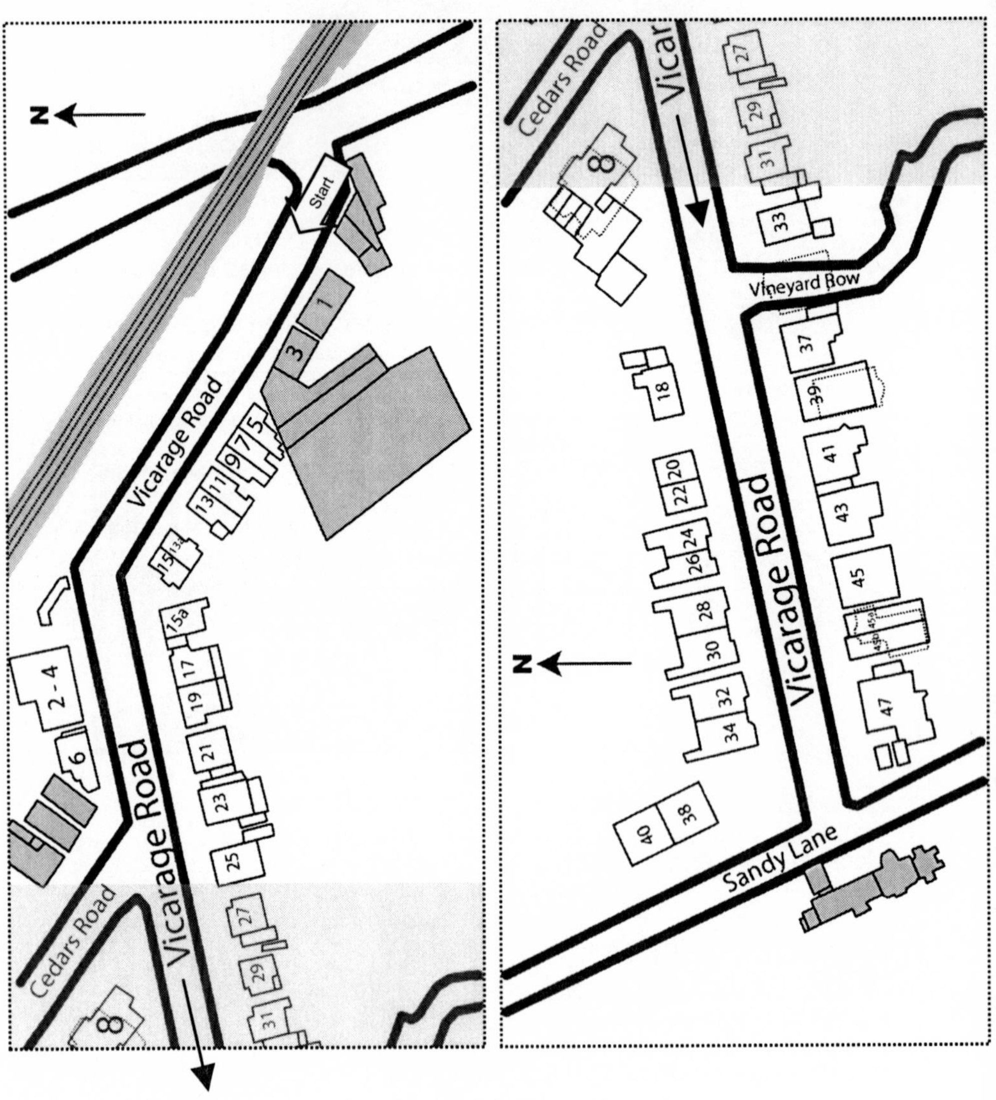

Vicarage Road
Start
Cedars Road
Vineyard Row
Sandy Lane
N

VICARAGE ROAD

Brick by Brick

Vicarage Road was first opened to the public in October 1883. It was principally created to provide access to the houses that were about to be built in the new Cedars Estate. However it also served as a road link between the High Street and Park Road and as a shortcut for those walking from the Railway Station to Bushy Park.

The Developer of the Cedars Estate originally proposed to call the thoroughfare Wolsey Road but the Local Board objected and insisted it be named Vicarage Road in recognition of the fact that the Parsonage stood at the junction of the new road with Park Road.

The Estate was divided into 62 building plots each 40 foot wide and, of these, 20 were located on Vicarage Road itself. "Only first-class residences of not less than £700 in value are to be erected upon them". However, by 1890 only seven houses had been built in the whole estate and the rules were relaxed.

above: **97a and 97b High Street**

Built in 1926 as an extension to Number 97, these shops have housed estate agents, confectioners, tobacconists, and a greengrocer. From 1982-2008, Number 97a was Bonzo's (a greasy spoon cafe) by day and, for a period, *Le Petit Max* (a high class French restaurant) by night.

above: ***The Cedars Works*, 1 and 3 Vicarage Road**

Laid out in 1886, this area has been used as an industrial estate ever since. The c.1904 photo of the New London Suburban Omnibus Company works with the yard full of horse buses awaiting conversion into motorised vehicles. Note the discarded wheels being carted away.

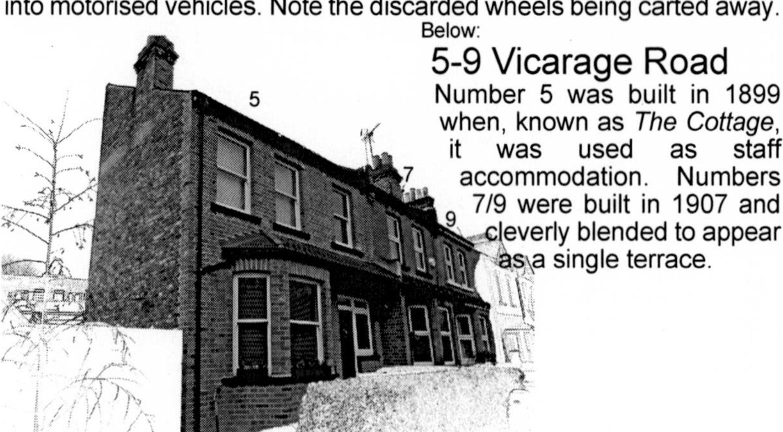

Below:

5-9 Vicarage Road

Number 5 was built in 1899 when, known as *The Cottage*, it was used as staff accommodation. Numbers 7/9 were built in 1907 and cleverly blended to appear as a single terrace.

above: **The Railway Embankment**

At this point the railway, having been steadily climbing from Teddington Station has reached the highest point on the line, ready to cross both Upper Teddington, Seymour and Lower Teddington Roads as well as the river crossing to the Kingston shore. The embankment was a very real barrier between east and west since Bushy Park Road was the only crossing point between Hampton Wick and Teddington Stations.

below: **Two possible Routes**

The original 1859 Bill for the Twickenham to Kingston Extension line proposed a southerly terminus at the foot of Kingston Bridge on the Middlesex side - on the site of The White Hart. There was considerable opposition from Kingston's would-be passengers who would have to cross the bridge (and pay a halfpenny toll) to board their train. A new Bill was presented with a river crossing into Kingston but necessitating the building of the embankment through the village.

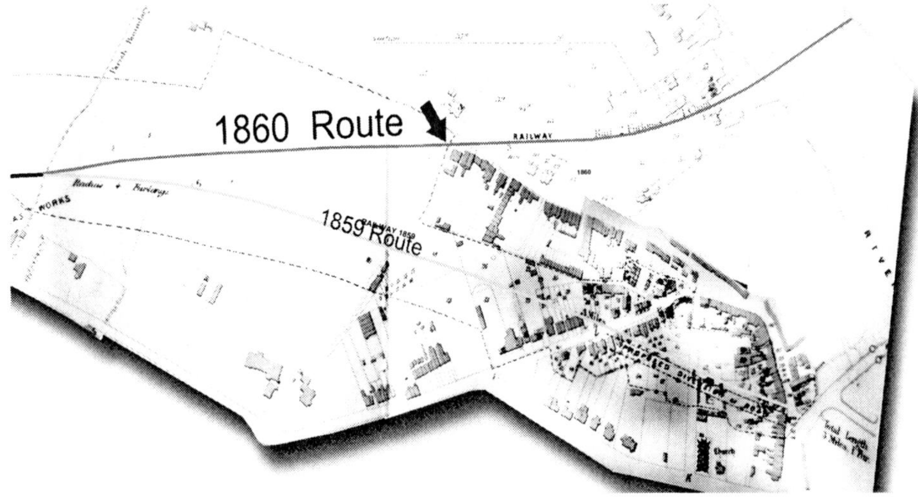

above: *Stoneywood and Fintray* ,
11/11a (now 13) Vicarage Road
Built in 1895, but over time the owners of these semi-detached properties have obviously disagreed whether they should have a canted or rounded bay and a round or pointed arch above the door.

above: 13a/19 Vicarage Road
Built in 1924 by the same developer using an identical lozenge motif on all the bay fronts.

below: *The Haven*, 21 Vicarage Road
Built in 1922 by Harold Fawcett, Clerk to Hampton Wick Urban District Council.

above: *Abigail Court* 2-4 Vicarage Road

Built around 2010 by Richmond Housing Trust on the site of *Cintra* and *Ellesmere.* The former was a large ten-room property which in 1906 was acquired by the Kingston Union Scattered Homes for Children. At the time of the 1911 Census and now called *Tudor Lodge*, the home housed 14 schoolgirls aged between 8 and 14. A similar home for 34 schoolboys was located at *Moira House* in Old Bridge Street.

below: *Ellesmere*, 6 Vicarage Road

Built in 1892 by Hezekiah Newman, who arrived in Hampton Wick as an agricultural labourer in the 1850s, later described himself as a dairyman and yet accumulated almost 20 properties in Hampton Wick of which, fittingly, *Ellesmere* was the most elaborate. In recent times the owners have sympathetically enlarged Hezekiah's original three-bay house by adding first a garage, then converting this into a playroom and finally adding a matching bay window to create today's totally-convincing four-bay structure.

Left, top to bottom:

23, 25 and 33 Vicarage Road

These three semi-bungalows were built in 1924, probably by the Offer family **[110]**. They display many Arts and Crafts elements including the prominent timbers and the lattice windows (not present in Number 33).

Left, top to bottom:

27-31 Vicarage Road

Built in 1926 also by the Offer family, these three houses share a bold design with its asymmetrical gable and the round arch above the recessed porch reflected in the brick feature above the main upstairs window. Number 31 recently added an extra two-storey bay, replacing the garage.

above: *Eisenhower House,* 8 Vicarage Road
Built in 1975, this 16-flat development was named to honour Gen. Dwight D Eisenhower who, as Supreme Allied Commander in Europe during World War 2, had his headquarters in Bushy Park during the early part of 1943.

below: *Carlogas*, 1 Cedars Road
Built in 1889 and designed by Irish architect Franc Sadleir Brereton, this 15-room mansion was demolished in 1975 to make way for *Eisenhower House*. Note Brereton's signature - the three small round arch clerestory windows in the gable - which also feature nearby on Number 3 Cedars Road as well as on Numbers 37, 41 and 45 Vicarage Road.

above: **The Missing Link**

The first houses on Vicarage Road were in this section of the road. Number 35 *Manor House* was demolished to provide the entrance for Vineyard Row.

above: *Keston Lodge and Holly Lodge* 37 and 41 Both built in 1885, and designed by architect Franc Sadleir Brereton, these were the first two of the five (almost) identical houses on The Cedars Estate.

below: *Lynwood and Woodcote* 43 and 45 Vicarage Road
Both built in 1889, Number 45 is identical to the earlier pair but Number 43 differs in some minor details particularly in the treatment of the eaves and the absence of the trademark clerestory windows on the gable.

above: **18 Vicarage Road**
Built in 1952 by Harry Viney. The total development included this house and two bungalows on Cedars Road built on a chevron-shaped plot that links the two roads. The land next to this property is an extension of the garden of Number 3 Cedars Road.

above: **20/22 Vicarage Road**
Built in 1933, its round bays and semi-circular recessed porches were typical of its time.

below: **24 and 26 Vicarage Road**
Built in 1960, and containing four separate residences but, since each has its own external door, these are not strictly flats but half-houses.

above left and right: **39a/b and 45a/b Vicarage Road**

Both newly built, these two developments have a lot in common: both occupy sites that had previously contained a bungalow and both employ so many styling elements of the Brereton designed houses either side of them that they thoroughly blend into the street.

below: ***Park Gate*, 47 Vicarage Road**

Park Gate was originally built in 1885 as one of the very first properties on Vicarage Road. According to the 1911 Census, it had 13 rooms - although only four people lived in it. The property remained virtually unchanged from wen it was built and had become dilapidated. At the time of writing, it has just been extensively refurbished with the exterior essentially unchanged from the original but the interior completely remodelled. Thus, happily, it again conforms with the ideals of Thomas Henry Burroughes - the original developer of The Cedars Estate - that "only first-class residences of not less than £700 in value are to be erected upon it".

above: *Braymead/Saratoga and Coningsby/Trethewy*

28/30 and 32/34 Vicarage Road

Built in 1904 and 1905 respectively, these two pairs of very substantial eight-room semi-detached houses differ only in minor details.

below: **36-42 Vicarage Road**

Well-concealed down a drive beside Number 34 and facing onto Sandy Lane, this development was built in 1962, originally as four flats. Number 40 has been combined with Number 42 to make a five-bedroom semi-detached house.

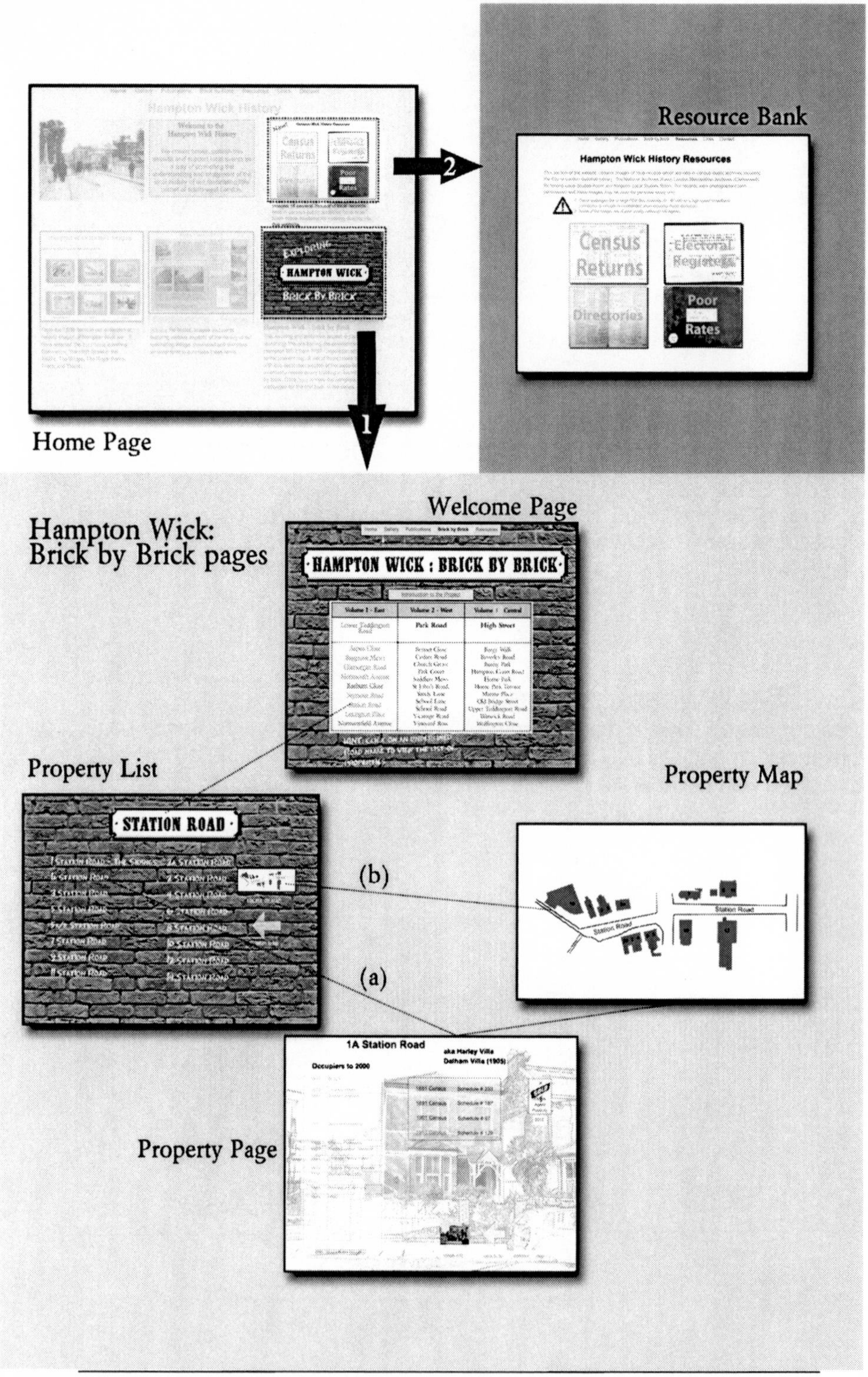

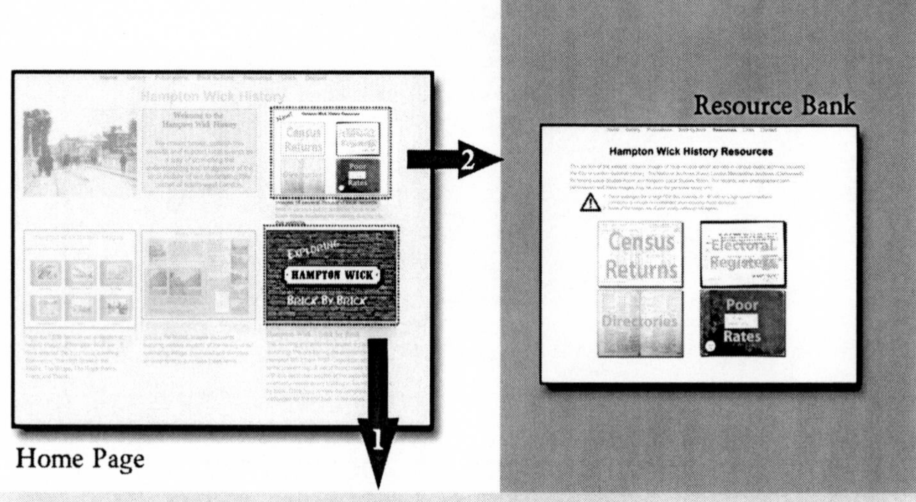

Welcome Page

Hampton Wick:
Brick by Brick pages

HAMPTON WICK : BRICK BY BRICK

Property List

STATION ROAD

Property Map

(b)

(a)

Station Road

1A Station Road

Occupiers to 2000

aka Harley Villa
Dalham Villa (1905)

Property Page

Appendix: THE BRICK BY BRICK WEBSITE

www.hamptonwickhistory.org.uk

Before starting to write this book, the author spent many happy hours and days researching in National and County Archives, in Local Study Rooms and on the Internet looking for material - data, maps, images, documents and articles - in fact, anything that would cast light on the development of Hampton Wick. Like any researcher, the task has then been to digest this large volume of material and extract the key facts and images to create this book's content in a (hopefully) interesting and entertaining format.

Normally, a researcher would then "park" the source material with possibly a bibliography and maybe a set of footnotes to point to the particular material used. However, it soon became clear that in this project *the source material itself* was potentially of as much value as the conclusions that had been drawn from it. Just as summary Census data tells us about overall population, so also can a particular set of individual Census entries provide snapshots of the occupants of a certain property over time.

The huge popularity of sites like *Ancestry.com* lies in the value that specific items within their vast collections can have for individuals conducting their own particular line of research. From these lines of thought stemmed two additional activities for the current project. First, to create and make available a collection of all the source material relating to the development of Hampton Wick. Second, to construct a mini-website (literally a homepage) for each residential property mentioned in this book containing (or pointing to) some of the key source material relating to that specific property. The output from both activities are included in the current website.

The website is an integral part of the overall ***Brick by Brick*** project. It has the potential to increase the value and enjoyment of this book for those readers who can take a moment to understand the structure and learn how to navigate their way around. The next few pages attempt to provide a brief guide to achieving this.

The diagram opposite shows how, from the ***Home Page*** of the main site, the user may click (1) to the ***Hampton Wick: Brick by Brick*** area of the site or (2) through to the ***Resource Bank***. The first option, when selected, opens a ***Welcome Page***. This presents the user with the contents of all three books as alphabetic lists of the streets covered in each (exactly as shown in the table on page 12). Clicking on an underlined street name (the underline signifies the existence of further information) leads to the **Property List**. From here the user may either (a) scroll down and directly select a property or (b) click on the miniature map for the option to browse and select off the **Property Map**. Either method leads to the **Property Page**.

Typical Property Page

Individual occupiers of this property (i.e. excluding flat dwellers) from the earliest available records. In accordance with accepted privacy standards, the list does not include householders from the last ten years.

The postal address of the property and whether it is designated as a National Heritage **Listed Building** or a London Borough of Richmond upon Thames Council **Building of Townscape Merit**.

aka: (Also Known As) Alternative names by which this property has been known. Dates of change are approximate and are usually based on the date that changes are noted in Census Return or a Street Directory.

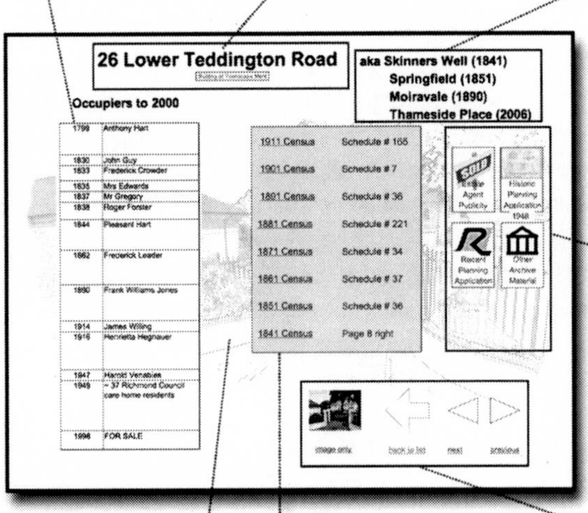

Icons in this area show there is other information available on this property. Typical items include slideshows from Estate Agents' publicity material relating to a recent sale or letting and extracts from planning applications - both historic (1890-1960) or recent (last ten years). Double-click on an icon to view the available material.

The background image is reproduced from the Brick by Brick section of the book. A full colour version can be viewed by clicking on the "Image only" in the Navigation Area of the screen (bottom right).

Census Returns - click to see the individual entries for this property. Use the schedule numbers to help locate on the Enumerator's sheet. 1911 Census Returns were completed by the occupier.

Navigation Area:
Click these buttons to view a full-screen image of the property, to return to the Property List page or to navigate to the next (i.e. higher numbered) or previous (i.e. lower numbered) property on this same side of the street.

Resource Bank

Clicking in the top right corner of the Home Page leads the user to this section of the website which contains images of local records which are held in various public archives including the City of London Guildhall Library, The National Archives (Kew), London Metropolitan Archives (Clerkenwell), Richmond Local Studies Room and Kingston Local Studies Room. The records were photographed (with permission) and these images may be used for personal study only.

The website carries the following two warnings:

a) These webpages link to large PDF files (typically 20-40 mB) so a high-speed broadband connection is strongly recommended when browsing these resources.
b) Some of the images are of poor quality (although still legible).

PLACE	HOUSES: Uninhabited or Building	HOUSES: Inhabited	NAMES of each Person who abode therein the preceding Night.	AGE and SEX: Males	AGE and SEX: Females	PROFESSION, TRADE, EMPLOYMENT, or of INDEPENDENT MEANS.	Whether Born in same County	Whether Born in Scotland, Ireland, or Foreign Parts
			Sarah Pearce		3[illegible]	F.S.	N	
		1	John Smith	30		M.S.	N	
Skinners Hall		1	Roger [illegible]	70		Ind.	Y	
			Mary do		60		Y	
			Jane do		20		N	
			Jane Jenkins		30		N	
			Harriet Watts		25		Y	
			Georgiana [illegible]		15		Y	
			[illegible] do		13		Y	
			Mary Jenkins		2		Y	
			Mary Mazzinghi		50		N	
			[illegible] do		60		N	
			Thomas do	25			N	
			Thomas John	25		Special Pleader	N	

above: 1841 Census - Enumerator's transcription
The first available Census records for Hampton Wick. Information was limited to name, gender, age, occupation. Note the entry for Skinners Hall which was the first recorded name for what is now known as *Thameside Place*.

below: 1891 Census - Enumerator's transcription
Additional information now includes the address of the property, the relationship to the Head of Family, occupation of all persons together with their place and year of birth.

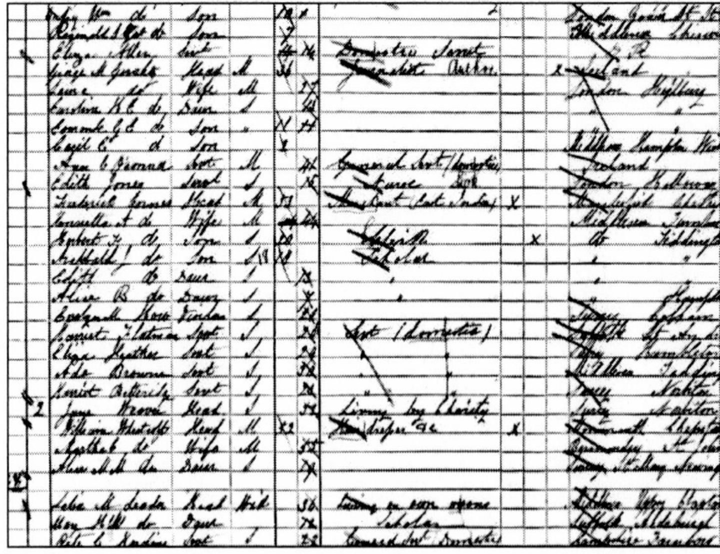

Census Returns 1841-1911

A full UK Census has been conducted every ten years since 1801 (excepting for 1941). The first four Censuses (1801–1831) were mainly headcounts and contained little personal information. In 1841, each householder was required to complete a Census schedule giving the address of the household, the names, ages, sex, occupations and places of birth of each individual residing in his or her accommodation. From 1851, householders were asked to give more precise details of the places of birth of each resident, to state their relationship to him or her, marital status and the nature of any disabilities from which they may have suffered. Census enumerators then collected the Census schedules and these were transcribed into Census enumerators' books. Although the original Census schedules were destroyed many years ago, the enumerators' books were kept. Census information is subject to a 100-year confidentiality period so the latest information available relates to the Census taken on 2 April 1911.

The Hampton Wick Census collection on the website contains complete returns for 1841 to 1901, with currently about one third of the returns for 1911.

below: **1911 Census - Householder's return**

The most recently available Census returns, and the first for which the original forms completed by the householder have been retained. Note how much more comprehensive is the information recorded - the inclusion of the number of rooms is particularly useful. This entry for "Rossendale" (Number 2 Seymour Road) includes playwright RC Sherriff, then a 14-year-old schoolboy at Kingston Grammar School.

NAME AND SURNAME	RELATIONSHIP to Head of Family	AGE (last Birthday) and SEX		PARTICULARS as to MARRIAGE					PROFESSION or OCCUPATION of Persons aged ten years and upwards
Of every Person, whether Member of Family, Visitor, Boarder, or Servant, who (1) passed the night of Sunday, April 2nd, 1911, in this dwelling and was alive at midnight, or (2) arrived in this dwelling on the morning of Monday, April 3rd, not having been enumerated elsewhere. No one else must be included. For order of entering names see Examples on back of Schedule.	State whether "Head," or "Wife," "Son," "Daughter," or other Relative, "Visitor," "Boarder," or "Servant."	For Infants under one year state the age in months as "under one month," "one month," etc. Ages of Males.	Ages of Females.	Write "Single," "Married," "Widower," or "Widow," opposite the names of all persons aged 15 years and upwards.	State, for each Married Woman entered on this Schedule, the number of:— Completed years the present Marriage has lasted. If less than one year write "under one."	Children born alive to present Marriage (If no children born alive write "None" in Column 7). Total Children Born Alive.	Children still Living.	Children who have Died.	Personal Occupation. The reply should show the precise branch of Profession, Trade, Manufacture, &c. If engaged in any Trade or Manufacture, the particular kind of work done, and the Article made or Material worked or dealt in should be clearly indicated. (See Instructions 1 to 8 and Examples on back of Schedule.)
Herbert H. Sherriff	Head	53		Married					Insurance Clerk
Annie C. Sherriff	Wife		38	Married	18	3	3	0	—
Beryl C. Sherriff	Daughter		18	Single					—
Robert C. Sherriff	Son	14		—					School
Cecil H. Sherriff	Son	11		—					School
Annie Pearce	Servant		23	Single		–	–	–	General Servant Domestic

Write below the Number of Rooms in this Dwelling (House, Tenement, or Apartment). Count the kitchen as a room but do not count scullery, landing, lobby, closet, bathroom; nor warehouse, office, shop.

Eleven

I declare that this Schedule is correctly filled up to the best of my knowledge and belief.

Signature Herbert H. Sherriff

Postal Address Rossendale, Seymour Rd Hampton Wick

No.	Christian Name and Surname of each Voter at full length.	Place of Abode.	Nature of Qualification.	Street, Lane, or other like Place in this Parish, and Number of House (if any), where the Property is situate, or Name of the Property, if known by any, or Name of the occupying Tenant; or if the Qualification consist of a Rent-charge, then the Names of the Owners of the Property out of which such Rent is issuing, or some of them, and the Situation of the Property.
		PARISH OF HAMPTON-WICK.—[1851-2.]		
190	Ashby, John	14, Old Compton-street	Freehold garden and shed	Occupied by Mrs. Minchin.
~~191~~	~~Babb, William~~	~~29, Upper Wharton-street, Lloyd-square, Pentonville, Middlesex~~	~~Two freehold houses~~	~~Adjoining the Swan public-house, in the Lower-road, and in the occupation of Thomas Kelly.~~
192	Beaman, George	Hampton Wick, and 32, King-street, Covent-garden	Freehold house and premises	In the occupation of Alexander Gordon, Esq.
193	Belchamber, Robert	Near the principal street, Hampton Wick, Middlesex	Freehold house and yard, &c.	Adjoining the road leading to Bushey Park, and also adjoining St. John's Cottages, and in my own occupation.
194	Bowyer, Frederick	London-road, Twickenham, Middlesex	Moiety of copyhold malthouse	Near the principal street, Hampton Wick, tenant Thomas Bowyer, jun.
195	Bowyer, Thomas	Guildford	Moiety of copyhold malthouse	Near the principal street, Hampton Wick.
196	Bunce, John	Teddington-row, Hampton Wick, Middlesex	Freehold house and garden	Teddington-road, Hampton Wick, occupied by myself and others.
197	Dale, Thomas	Park-lane, Hampton Wick	Freehold house	Albion House, Park-lane, Hampton Wick, occupied by myself.
198	Earl, John	Kingston-on-Thames, Surrey	Freehold house and yard	Situate in Hampton Wick, Middlesex, occupied by widow Bishop.
199	Elmore, John Richard	27, Harley-street, London	Copyhold estate and freehold held in right of my wife	The Cedars, occupying tenant John Guy, Esq.; and Thorpe Farm, occupying tenant Mrs. Sarah Salter Minchin, being freehold and copyhold estates.
200	Feltham, James	East Moulsey	Copyhold houses	Occupied by Headland.
201	Fenner, Charles James	Hampton Wick	Freehold house	Occupied by himself.

above: **1851-2 Hampton Wick Electoral Register**

The right to vote was restricted to males who owned or leased property worth more than a specified value. A system of registration was administered by the overseers of the poor. Individual's claims for voting rights were entered in a printed register. The entries were then vetted - and could be overruled - by the overseer (as in entry #191 above). Entry 192 refers to *Rivermead* (6 Lower Teddington Road) and 201 to *Park House* on Park Road. Entry 199 refers to two houses and a large area of land which eventually became the site of Vicarage and Cedars Roads.

below: **1894 Hampton Wick Electoral Register**

From this year, women who owned property could vote in local elections.

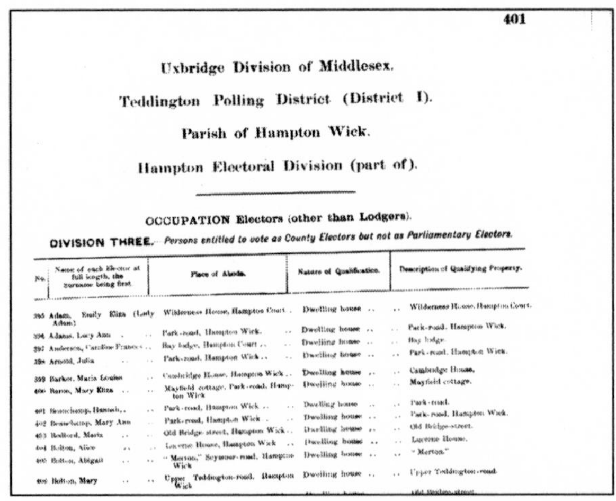

401

Uxbridge Division of Middlesex.

Teddington Polling District (District I).

Parish of Hampton Wick.

Hampton Electoral Division (part of).

OCCUPATION Electors (other than Lodgers).

DIVISION THREE. *Persons entitled to vote as County Electors but not as Parliamentary Electors.*

No.	Name of each Elector at full length, the surname being first	Place of Abode.	Nature of Qualification.	Description of Qualifying Property.
395	Adam, Emily Eliza (Lady Adam)	Wilderness House, Hampton Court	Dwelling house	Wilderness House, Hampton Court.
396	Adams, Lucy Ann	Park-road, Hampton Wick	Dwelling house	Park-road, Hampton Wick.
397	Anderson, Caroline Frances	Bay lodge, Hampton Court	Dwelling house	Bay lodge.
398	Arnold, Julia	Park-road, Hampton Wick	Dwelling house	Park-road, Hampton Wick.
399	Barker, Maria Louisa	Cambridge House, Hampton Wick	Dwelling house	Cambridge House.
400	Baron, Mary Eliza	Mayfield cottage, Park-road, Hampton Wick	Dwelling house	Mayfield cottage.
401	Beauchamp, Hannah	Park-road, Hampton Wick	Dwelling house	Park-road.
402	Beauchamp, Mary Ann	Park-road, Hampton Wick	Dwelling house	Park-road, Hampton Wick.
403	Bedford, Maria	Old Bridge-street, Hampton Wick	Dwelling house	Old Bridge-street.
404	Bolton, Alice	Lucerne House, Hampton Wick	Dwelling house	Lucerne House.
405	Bolton, Abigail	"Merton," Seymour-road, Hampton Wick	Dwelling house	"Merton."
406	Bolton, Mary	Upper Teddington-road, Hampton Wick	Dwelling house	Upper Teddington-road.

Electoral Registers

Electoral registers are lists of voters able to vote in parliamentary and local government elections. They are arranged by constituency and divided into polling districts. Electoral registration was introduced by the Reform Act of 1832 and, since then, registers have been compiled annually with the exception of the years 1916, 1917 and 1940 to 1944. The original Act directed parish overseers to prepare the electoral registers which were compiled from returns. Rules for who was allowed to vote were defined in the various Representation of the People Acts significant amongst which were the Acts of 1918 (all men over 21 and women over 30 allowed to vote), 1928 (women over 21) and 1969 (voting age reduced to 18).

The website collection of Electoral Registers for Hampton Wick includes the Overseers' Returns from 1847-1882 (complete with their handwritten corrections and deletions) together with the actual registers from 1883-1899 and from 1945-2000. The image quality of some of the registers from 1940 on is marginal.

below: **1945 Hampton Wick Electoral Register**
The modern register is a simple listing of eligible voters with their postal addresses.

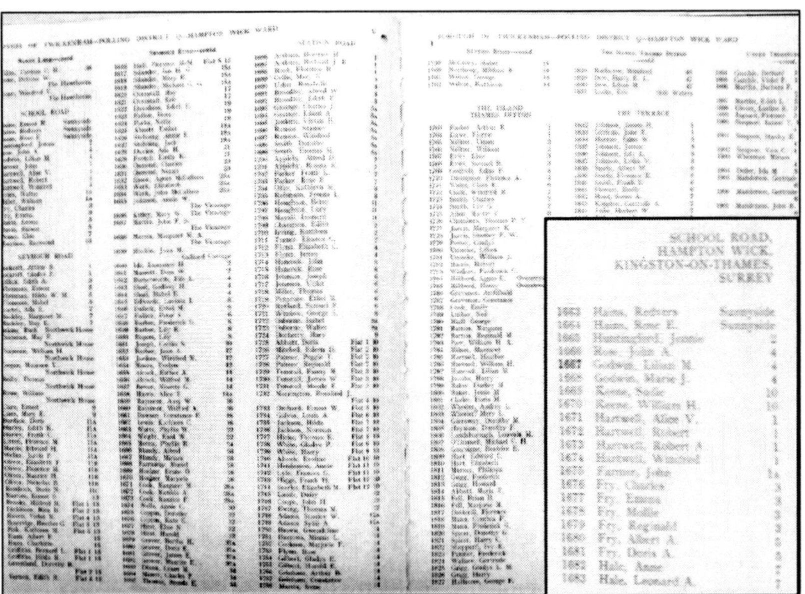

SCHOOL ROAD,
HAMPTON WICK,
KINGSTON-ON-THAMES,
SURREY

1663	Hams, Redvers	Sunnyside
1664	Hams, Rose E.	Sunnyside
1665	Huntingford, Jennie	2
1666	Rose, John A.	4
1667	Godwin, Lilian M.	4
1668	Godwin, Marie J.	4
1669	Keene, Sadie	10
1670	Keene, William H.	10
1671	Hartwell, Alice V.	1
1672	Hartwell, Robert	1
1673	Hartwell, Robert A.	1
1674	Hartwell, Winifred	1
1675	Farmer, John	1a
1676	Fry, Charles	3
1677	Fry, Emma	3
1678	Fry, Mollie	3
1679	Fry, Reginald	3
1680	Fry, Albert A.	5
1681	Fry, Doris A.	5
1682	Hale, Anne	7
1683	Hale, Leonard A.	7

Middlesex, &c. HAMPTON, &c. Pigot & Co.'s

Griffinhoofe Mrs. Hampton
Halliday Sir Andw. M. D. Hampton Court
Hallifax Miss, Hampton
Hardwick Ts. esq. Hampton Court
Harvey Lister, esq. New Hampton
Hase Henry, esq. Hampton
Hawkes Mrs. New Hampton
Hawkins Miss, Hampton Court
Hemming Rev. Sml. DD. Hampton
Hennington Benjamin, esq. Hampton Court
Herbert —, esq. Hampton Wick
Herder Joel, esq. New Hampton
Hetherington Mrs. HamptonCourt
Hodson —, esq. Hampton
Holloway Mrs. Hampton Wick
Hulme Arden, esq. HamptonWick
Jesse Edwd. esq. Hampton Wick
Kempf —, esq. Hampton
Kensett Fras. esq. Hampton Wick
King John, esq. Hampton
Kirkman C. F. esq. HamptonWick
Lansdown Dowager Marchioness, Hampton Court
Langharne —, MD. HamptonWick
Lavington Hon. Lady, Hampton Court Palace
Legh Mrs. Hampton Court
Linfield Mrs. Hampton Wick
Ludlow Hon. Lady Ann, Hampton Court Palace

Tolmash Lady Laura, Hanworth
Turner Joseph, esq. Hampton
Twining John, esq. Hampton
Vesey Mrs. Hampton CourtPalace
Walker Mrs. HamptonCourtPalace
Wallis Mrs. Hampton
Walpole Misses, Hampton Court Palace
Warburton Miss, Hampton Court
Wheatley Lt.-Col. HamptonCourt
Whitshed Admiral Sir Jas. Hawkins, Hampton Court Palace
Wightman —, esq. Hampton
Willis Mrs. Hampton Court Palace
Wise Miss, Hampton
Woolmore John, esq. Hampton
Worley —, esq. Hampton Court
Wright Mrs. Barbara, Hampton Court Palace
Wright Robert, esq. Hampton Court Palace
Wyndham Mrs. Hampton Court
Yeo Misses, Hampton Court Palace
Yonge Lady, Hampton
Young John, esq. Hampton Court Palace

ACADEMIES.

Barnes Ryley, (gent's day) Hampton Wick
Berryman and Francis, (ladies' boarding) Hampton
Berryman Mrs. (gent's prepara-

Collins Richard, Hampton Wick
Farrant John, (and builder & undertaker) Hanworth
Gill Joseph, New Hampton
Mansell Hannah, Hampton
Murray John, Hampton Court
Walker James, Hampton Wick

COAL MERCHANTS.

Bagnoll Robert, New Hampton
Benn Thos. Hampton
CollinsJn.Maycock, Hampton wick
Kensett Fredk. Hampton Court

CORN DEALERS.

Benn Thos. Hampton
Newbery John, Hampton Court
Richardson Thos. Henry, Hampton Wick
Wells Charles, Hampton

EARTHENWARE DEALRS

Abbett Thomas, Hampton
Newberry Mrs. Hampton

FISHMONGERS.

Coombes Richard, Hampton
Ruff Henry, Hampton

FRUITERERS.

Herbert Wm. Hampton Court
Singleton George, Hampton

GROCERS AND CHEESEMONGERS.

Carpenter Thos. Hampton
Downton James, Hampton
Evans Robert, Hampton Wick

above: Pigot's 1826 Middlesex Directory
At this time, individuals and Traders paid for their entries in the directory. The academy listed as being run by Ryley Barnes was in Number 3 Lower Teddington Road.

below: Green's 1888 Directory of Hampton Wick
This unique local directory was produced by R Green, printer, stationer and bookbinder of Caxton House (now 47 High Street) Hampton Wick.
(Transcription courtesy of Paul Barnfield)

CHURCH GROVE
From Hampton Court Road to junction with Park Road

Durnford, H.M., esq., The Pines
Fawssett, Rev. R., Fairlight
PARISH CHURCH
here is St. John's Road
House unoccupied
Ferguson, R.F.,esq., The Nest
Wilkinson, W.M., esq., The Limes
Brown, A., esq., The Bays
Wild, Mrs., Suffolk Lodge
Oldham, T., esq., Woodville
Watts, H.W., esq., Bushey Villa
Thompson, W., esq., Hope Cottage
BETLEY VILLAS
Taylor, S., esq.
Whenman, T., jun.
Brown, Mrs.
here is Park Road.

Trade and Street Directories

Directories are an invaluable primary source for historians. They provide first hand data about local communities, their infrastructure and the individuals inhabiting those communities. Published more frequently than the Census, directories can also help fill in any missing gaps. Early directory compilers often relied on people sending in their names together with a small payment if they wanted to be included in the directory. By growing links with the Post Office, the compilers were able to use information originally gathered for mail-delivery purposes. Best known was Frederick Festus Kelly whose eponymous directories first appeared in 1845. They continued in production until the early 1970's, at which time the Kelly's HQ was in Tudor House, Hampton Wick.

This current website collection includes twenty Trade Directories covering the period 1826-1886. A one-off locally-produced directory was published by E Green of 47 High Street in 1888 (thanks to Paul Barnfield who has painstakingly transcribed it). There also is a complete set of Kelly's Directories covering the period 1892-1940 when Hampton Wick was dropped from Kelly's coverage.

below: Kelly's 1938 Directory of Hampton Wick
One of the last directories covering Hampton Wick.

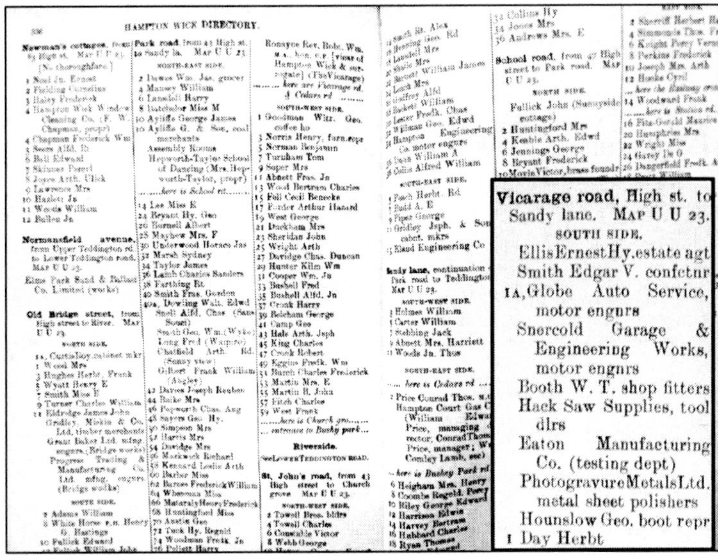

HAMPTON WICK DIRECTORY.

Vicarage road, High st. to Sandy lane. MAP U U 23.

SOUTH SIDE.

Ellis Ernest Hy. estate agt
Smith Edgar V. confectnr
1A, Globe Auto Service, motor engnrs
Snercold Garage & Engineering Works, motor engnrs
Booth W. T. shop fitters
Hack Saw Supplies, tool dlrs
Eaton Manufacturing Co. (testing dept)
PhotogravureMetalsLtd. metal sheet polishers
Hounslow Geo. boot repr
1 Day Herbt

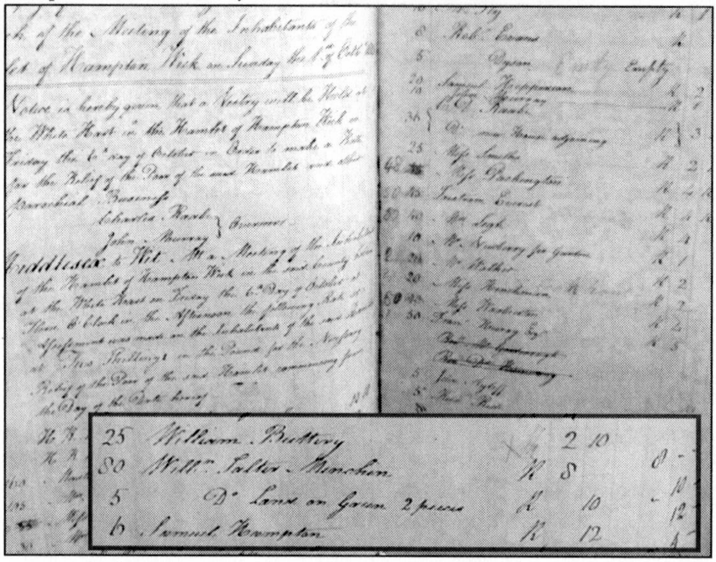

above: **Hampton Wick Poor Rates Book 1808**
This image from the earliest Poor Rates Book available shows the minimalism in the accounting system. Almost all payments were identified just by name, with only an occasional note of the property to which it referred.

below: **Hampton Wick Poor Rates Book 1868**
By this date, the records included the name of the occupier as well as owner together with brief description of the property. The entries were in street order although no street numbering was yet in existence.

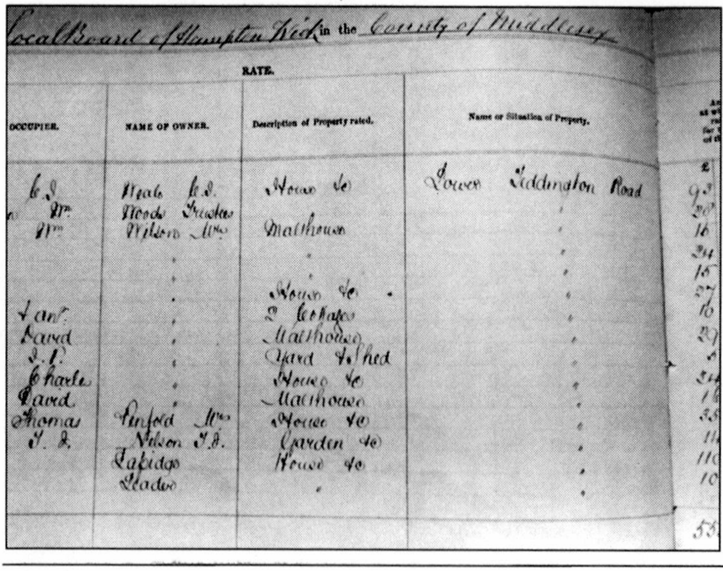

Poor Rates Books

The Poor Law - originating from the reign of Elizabeth I - created a system for the relief of the Poor, administered at parish level and paid for by levying local rates on property owners and middle-class occupiers. Each Parish elected two Overseers of the Poor annually who were responsible for setting the Poor Rates, collecting the dues and distributing the proceeds to the Poor. They were answerable to two Justices of the Peace for the County for the correct administration of the system. The combination of skills and attributes needed to be an effective Overseer meant that in practice the same limited group of individuals performed the task in rotation.

The rates as collected were recorded into Poor Rates Books, the earliest available for Hampton Wick being a standard format accounts book dating from 1808 and listing names, rateable values and amount collected. A comprehensive reform and centralisation of the Poor Law System in 1834 created standardised books which recorded both occupier and owner and included a description of the property. When the Hampton Wick Local Board promulgated street names in 1864, this was added to the information recorded in the Poor Rates Books, greatly increasing their value to the researcher. Roughly one-third of the original set of Hampton Wick Poor Rates books survive from the period 1808 to 1915 and are included on the website.

below: **Hampton Wick Poor Rates Book 1915**
The last book that has survived, all entries now include street addresses.

			RATE.
[...] of Occupier.	Name of Owner.	Description of Property Rated.	Name or Situation of Property Rated.
1	2	3	4
Matthew	Thames Conservators	Manor Garden	Barge Walk The Wilderness
	Himself	do	Sorkford
	Halfhide Alfd Edward	Shop	1 Home Park Terrace
Ellen	"		2
	"	"	3
Frank Bean	"	"	4
		"	5
	"	Navy Station Yard	
	Mary Trustees		Old Bridge Street

Other Books in the Hampton Wick History Series by Ray Elmitt

A Hampton Wick Timeline - from Domesday to Current Day (November 2010)

A collection of thirty-one images from photographs, postcards, maps and news-cuttings telling the illustrated story of this historic village in south-west London. Each picture is provided with a caption that sets the historic context and which, collectively, provide a brief but thorough history of Hampton Wick.

66pp (150 x 230 mm) perfect bound b&w £6.99 ISBN 978-0-9571679-0-2

The High Street Traders of Hampton Wick (May 2011)

A fascinating study of Hampton Wick High Street which, although less than 400 metres long, has in its time been host to more than seventy shops and pubs. In this comprehensive review of the period from 1826 to the current day, the author has traced every retail establishment, listing the shop-keepers and their trades and providing a series of reminiscences and anecdotes extracted from several sets of local memoirs as well as the more than twenty five interviews he has conducted during his research. Illustrated with over 500 photographs, maps and contemporary adverts.

178 pp (150 x 230 mm) perfect bound black and white £9.99 ISBN 978-0-9571679-2-6

Hampton Wick: Brick by Brick
Volume 1 Lower Teddington Road and environs (October 2012)

Hampton Wick lies in a strategic position on the River Thames. For five hundred years its bridge was the only fixed crossing between London and Staines. Its connections with the ancient town of Kingston on the opposite bank and the presence of the nearby Royal Palace of Hampton Court brought prosperity and the village grew from a hamlet of around 500 souls in 1750 to a peak of 3,400 in 1951.

The *Hampton Wick: Brick by Brick* series of three books explores this fascinating period of rapid urban development. Volume 1 covers the east of the village and is written in two distinct parts:

- The first section recounts the history of the building of the village: who owned the land? who built the roads and houses? who lived in them? how have the buildings been altered and extended over time?
- The second section focuses on today's Hampton Wick and provides a set of walking guides to encourage readers to explore for themselves the wealth of interest in the more than eight hundred buildings that now form the village.

"The most breathtakingly comprehensive local history project I have ever encountered"
June Sampson Richmond & Twickenham Times 17 May 2013

178 pp (150 x 230 mm) perfect bound black and white £9.99 ISBN 978-0-9571679-3-3

For more information and to order visit www.hamptonwickhistory.org.uk or write to:
1 *The Grove*, 24 Lower Teddington Road, Hampton Wick, Middlesex KT1 4HJ